LEGAL REASON

Legal Reason describes and explains the process of analogical reasoning, which is the distinctive feature of legal argument. It challenges the prevailing view, urged by Edward Levi, Cass Sunstein, Richard Posner, and others, which regards analogical reasoning as logically flawed or as a defective form of deductive reasoning. It shows that analogical reasoning in the law is the same as the reasoning used by all of us routinely in everyday life and that it is a valid form of reasoning derived from the innate human capacity to recognize the general in the particular, on which thought itself depends. The use of analogical reasoning is dictated by the nature of law, which requires the application of rules to particular facts. Written for scholars as well as students, practitioners, and persons who are generally interested in law, *Legal Reason* is written in clear, accessible prose, with many examples drawn from the law and everyday experience.

Lloyd L. Weinreb is Dane Professor of Law at Harvard Law School. He is the author of *Natural Law and Justice* and *Oedipus at Fenway Park: What Rights Are and Why There Are Any.*

Legal Reason

THE USE OF ANALOGY IN LEGAL ARGUMENT

LLOYD L. WEINREB

Harvard Law School

CAMBRIDGE
UNIVERSITY PRESS

CAMBRIDGE UNIVERSITY PRESS
Cambridge, New York, Melbourne, Madrid, Cape Town, Singapore, São Paulo

Cambridge University Press
40 West 20th Street, New York, NY 10011-4211, USA

www.cambridge.org
Information on this title: www.cambridge.org/9780521849678

First published 2005

Printed in the United States of America

A catalog record for this book is available from the British Library.

Library of Congress Cataloging in Publication Data
Weinreb, Lloyd L., 1936–
Legal reason : the use of analogy in legal argument / Lloyd L. Weinreb.
p. cm.
Includes bibliographical references and index.
ISBN 0-521-84967-5 (casebound) – ISBN 0-521-61490-2 (pbk.)
1. Law–Methodology. I. Title.
K213.W45 2005
340'.11 – dc22 2004023974

ISBN-13 978-0-521-84967-8 hardback
ISBN-10 0-521-84967-5 hardback

ISBN-13 978-0-521-61490-0 paperback
ISBN-10 0-521-61490-2 paperback

Contents

Preface

Recent discussions of the use of analogy in legal argument, which measure its use against the standards of deductive and inductive reasoning and find it wanting, prompted me to write this book. Even those who have approved the use of analogical argument in the law, like Edward Levi in his classic study, *An Introduction to Legal Argument*, have thought it is rationally "flawed," although how in that case it could have the benign effects that Levi and others attribute to it is not explained. So also, efforts to reconstruct analogical legal argument as only a slightly disguised form of deductive or inductive argument, or some combination of the two, distort the arguments that lawyers and judges actually make and are evidently dictated only by the conviction that otherwise the arguments are invalid and entitled to no weight.

Views of this kind, which have dominated the discussion about analogical legal reasoning, fly in the face of the indubitable fact that the use of analogy is at the very center of legal reasoning, so much so that it is regarded as an identifying characteristic not only of legal reasoning itself but also of legal education. It is simply not credible that arguments subjected routinely to the closest scrutiny would contain such fundamental error. Studying the matter, I confirmed my belief that the use of analogical argument in law stands up on its own terms and is not different from the reasoning on which we all rely in the affairs of everyday life. Its

Preface

use in the law is distinct only in that it is not merely commonplace and useful but is essential to preservation of values that we ascribe to "the rule of law." The effort to displace analogical reasoning by deductive or inductive reasoning responds to a mistaken belief that the rule of law so requires. Analogical reasoning does not undermine the rule of law but rather sustains it.

I intend this book both for those who are interested in the scholarly debate and those who are beginning their legal studies or just entering the practice of law, as well as persons who have a general interest in law. Addressing myself to these audiences, I have not scanted discussion of the issues. I have, however, omitted most of the apparatus – lengthy footnotes about marginally relevant points and extensive citation – that is, excessively I think, common to legal scholarship. I have been generous with commonplace examples and with explanations of matters that will be familiar to legal scholars and experienced practitioners but perhaps not to beginning students, practitioners starting out, and others outside the legal profession.

I am grateful to many colleagues and friends who read some or all of the manuscript and made fruitful suggestions, among whom are Brian Bix, Michael Doyen, Richard Fallon, Robert Ferguson, Morton Horwitz, Daniel Meltzer, Anton Metlitsky, Daniel Weinreb, Mark Yohalem, and Benjamin Zipursky.

Andrew Waterhouse, George Borg, and Marcia Chapin helped me to understand the chemistry of wine stains and talcum powder. I presented some of the ideas in the book at workshops at Cornell Law School, Fordham Law School, and Harvard Law School and was encouraged and stimulated by comments of the participants.

The library of Harvard Law School provided ready access to books and articles about a wide variety of subjects, including many that did not make it into the final manuscript. The library of Fordham Law School was similarly helpful when I was a visiting professor there in 2003. Melinda Eakin prepared and managed many drafts of the manuscript and assisted in the final copyediting. Her help was invaluable. Ed Parsons was a generous and helpful representative of Cambridge University Press.

Lloyd L. Weinreb
October 2004

Introduction

This is a book about the arguments that lawyers make in support of their clients and judges make in the course of their opinions. That is not the whole of the law, which extends in every direction and takes many different forms. The pattern of reasoning of those who are engaged elsewhere in the law, in the legislative process or in the regulatory or administrative process, is different. But adjudication, in which lawyers' arguments and judicial opinions hold sway, is typically the place where the law is brought to bear concretely and, to use a current expression, "the rubber hits the road." No effort to understand and explain the law or the legal process can succeed unless the arguments of lawyers and judges are understood. Those arguments, furthermore, are what people have in mind when they speak about legal reasoning. It is widely believed that legal reasoning is somehow special, not just in its subject matter but in its very form. In a law school class, a professor, intending high praise, may say to a student, "Now you are thinking like a lawyer," as if a legal education equips a person to think in a way unknown to others. And, indeed, a great deal has been written about the nature of legal arguments.[1] Yet it would be odd if legal reasoning were somehow different from reasoning about other subjects. Doctors and engineers also have their special expertise. One does not hear so much talk about thinking like a doctor or thinking like an engineer.

There is a large difference in one respect between the practice of law and other professions, which surely has something to do with the special attention given to legal reasoning. The reasoning of a doctor or an engineer is readily and in the normal course put to the test. The patient's health improves, or it does not; the bridge stands, or it falls. There is no comparable test of legal reasoning. Although we talk about what the law is, as though it is a matter of fact like a medical diagnosis or the weight a bridge will support, the content of the law is normative: It prescribes what is – that is to say, ought – to be done. (Even to say that it declares what will be done is too much; for there are many instances when the law is not followed.) How to resolve that conjunction of what is and what ought to be is one of the fundamental problems of jurisprudence. Because the outcome of legal reasoning does not furnish an objective test of its merit, it is unsurprising that we attend more insistently to the process of reasoning itself.

The stakes are large. For the law provides an overarching structure within which most human affairs are conducted, and it reaches down to the smallest details. If its demands are not to be felt as arbitrary and oppressive, they must be, and must be perceived to be, reasonable. Whatever may be the grounds for the authority of law in general or of a particular law or body of law on a specific subject, when the law takes hold and determines specific rights and obligations of specific persons, its justification characteristically is found in the arguments of lawyers and judges. On the face of it, the analysis of legal reasoning, which is subjected to close, persistent, and thorough scrutiny, should be straightforward. Lawyers' arguments are rebutted by arguments of lawyers on the other side. When a judge decides a case, he has an opportunity to explain his decision and may be required to do so. The decision ordinarily can be appealed to a higher court, where it is reviewed by a panel of judges, whose decision also is generally explained on the record. Often that decision can be appealed to still another court and another panel. The pattern of such argument, its merits and defects, are, one would think, unusually open to view. Yet the amount that has been written about legal reasoning and the diversity of views suggest otherwise, as if it is not what it appears to be or is subject to some demand that direct examination does not satisfy.

There is something distinctive about legal reasoning, which is its reliance on analogy. Leaving more precise definition for later, an analogical argument can be described as reasoning by example: finding the solution to a problem by reference to another similar problem and its solution. Reasoning of this kind is by no means unique to the law; on the contrary, it is the way all of us respond to countless ordinary problems in everyday life. Nor do analogical arguments displace other forms of reasoning about law, when they are appropriate. Analogical arguments are, however, especially prominent in legal reasoning, so much so that they are regarded as its hallmark. And, as a hallmark, they are not reassuring. Although the value of an analogy as a figure of speech is acknowledged, the value is commonly thought to belong to the art of persuasion and not to reason. Analogical arguments are said to be slippery and likely to mislead or, at any rate, not to be firm enough to support a seriously contested conclusion. They are contrasted in this respect with deductive and inductive arguments. A deductive argument is subject to the rules of formal logic. According to those rules, an argument is either valid or invalid, and there is no more to be said one way or the other. An inductive argument is not formally bound in the same way; but the conclusion can be tested experimentally, and, again, either it is verified, or it is not. The similarity at the heart of an analogical argument, on the other hand, does not display its significance, as a deductive argument displays its validity. Things (or persons, or events) are similar and dissimilar to one another and to all sorts of other things in countless ways, all at the same time. There simply are no rules that prescribe how much or what sort of similarity is enough to sustain analogies generally or to sustain a particular analogy. Nor can an analogy be tested experimentally, for the similarity on which it depends may be unquestioned but have nothing to do with the conclusion that is said to follow from it, whether the conclusion be true or false.

For all the prominence of analogical arguments in the actual reasoning of lawyers and judges, they are largely disregarded in the theoretical model of legal reasoning that, explicitly or implicitly, pervades legal analysis. According to that model, legal reasoning is built of determinate rules linked by logical inference, the correctness of which can, at least in principle, be ascertained. The model is familiarly represented as a pyramid, decisions in concrete cases at the base being derived from a rule, which in turn is derived from a higher rule and so on, up to the highest of all, from which all the rest are derived, at the apex.* Alternatively, the most fundamental rule forms

---

* Much has been made in jurisprudential literature about the difference between rules and principles. Ronald Dworkin developed the distinction in his article *The*

the base of the pyramid, each rule above resting on the one beneath, up to the decision in a case at the apex.*

Few people suppose anymore, as was once maintained, that scrupulous adherence to this model is all that is required to reach the correct result; indeed, whether there is, in that sense, a correct result is contentious.[2] But our inability to demonstrate the truth of a judicial decision as if it were a mathematical proof is commonly perceived as a practical limitation attributable to the fractious subject matter, rather than a flaw in the model itself. The proper method of arriving at a decision is said to be to set forth the relevant rules, resolve any inconsistencies among them, and bring them collectively

---

Model of Rules, 35 U. Chi. L. Rev. 14 (1967), reprinted in Ronald Dworkin, *Taking Rights Seriously* 14–45 (1977). For a helpful (skeptical) discussion of the distinction, see Frederick Schauer, *Prescriptions in Three Dimensions*, 82 Iowa L. Rev. 911 (1997). The difference between rules, which, generally speaking, provide a determinate response to specific facts, and standards, which call for consideration of all the circumstances, has also been much discussed. See, e.g., Duncan Kennedy, *Form and Substance in Private Law Adjudication*, 89 Harv. L. Rev. 1685, 1687–1713 (1976); Kathleen M. Sullivan, *Foreword, The Justices of Rules and Standards*, 106 Harv. L. Rev. 24, 56–123 (1992). Whatever importance these distinctions may have, they have no relevance here. I frequently refer to "rules" as including rules, principles, and standards.

* Whether the law is constructed from the top down or from the bottom up is a matter of considerable importance, see pp. 140–142, although that is usually left out of account in the construction of the metaphorical pyramid, which is left to the individual imagination. It has not escaped notice, however, that either way, the pyramid does not stand on its own and requires external scaffolding. For the dependence of rule on rule must come to an end somewhere. If the pyramid is built top down, there seems to be nothing holding up the apex; and if it is built bottom up, the base seems itself to rest on air. Providing a skyhook for the apex or a foundation for the base is the perennial task of jurisprudence. See pp. 154–160.

to a coherent focus on the facts of the case. Ronald Dworkin, for example, has forcefully defended the thesis that in order to reach the right answer, a judge has to bring his decision "within some comprehensive theory of general principles and policies that is consistent with other decisions also thought right"; it must be "consistent with earlier decisions not recanted, and with decisions that the institution is prepared to make in the hypothetical circumstances."*3 Evoking the familiar image of a pyramid, Dworkin says that this comprehensive theory must have "a vertical and a horizontal ordering": vertical, inasmuch as a justificatory principle must be "consistent with principles taken to provide the justification of higher levels," and horizontal, inasmuch as it "must also be consistent with the justification offered for other decisions at that level."4 Elsewhere, he has described the process of decision as a "justificatory ascent."5 Dworkin does not suppose that a judge will often accomplish so arduous a task or even that he will often be tempted to try. Famously, he named his exemplary judge "Hercules."6 Many scholars, furthermore, without denying that a judge is obligated to decide according to the law, have questioned whether the full scope of that obligation can be contained in articulable principles. The resort to principle, however, so far as it goes, and the model of legal reasoning

---

* Information about legal scholars and others whose views are discussed in the text is given in Appendix B.

as a hierarchical order of rules subject to a requirement of vertical and horizontal consistency are not generally questioned, practically or theoretically.* It is evident that analogical arguments do not conform to this model. Rather than composing a pyramid of rules held together by deductive inference, the arguments of lawyers and judges resemble a Tinker-toy construction, one case being linked to another by factual similarities that are deemed to warrant application of the same rule.

Confronted by this discrepancy between the theoretical model and the palpable fact that analogical arguments abound, legal scholars have drawn a variety of conclusions. Some affirm a hierarchy of rules as the officially correct model but urge that room be made for analogical arguments as well. Despite their logical weakness, or, indeed, because of it, these

---

* An important strand of twentieth-century American jurisprudence questions more fundamentally whether adjudication is principled in the manner that the model suggests. The Legal Realist school of jurisprudence, prominent in the 1930s, and the Critical Legal Studies school, prominent in the 1980s, asserted that the rules on which courts purport to rely are a mask for what are essentially political decisions: there is not a clear separation between legislation and adjudication, and judges, consciously or not, conform the results that they reach to policies determined otherwise. Although the arguments of the Realists and "Crits," as they are called, are a valuable corrective to simplistic assertions that rules in and of themselves dictate their application to concrete cases, the wholesale rejection of the force of rules is unconvincing. The Realists and Crits made their case only by misconceiving or disregarding entirely the role of analogical reasoning in making rules work. They thus fell into the same trap, albeit to contrary effect, as the legal formalists whose theories they derided. See pp. 140–142.

scholars urge, analogical arguments serve a useful function by promoting the settlement of difficult cases. So, in his classic study of legal reasoning, Edward Levi observed that analogical argument is "imperfect" and contains a "logical fallacy."* Nevertheless, he said, it is the "basic pattern of legal reasoning" and is "indispensable to peace in a community," because it is the means by which the law grows and changes in conformity with the community's views, even as it is being applied.[7] Levi's confidence that the adjudicative process helps to preserve "peace in a community" may seem misplaced today, when judicial decisions on issues like abortion, gay rights, and affirmative action are as likely to divide the community as to unite it and judicial appointments are a potent political issue. But in any case, his concession that analogical reasoning is logically flawed leaves one to wonder whether peace is not obtained at too high a price. Others are more skeptical of the virtues of analogical arguments and believe that they are used a great deal too much. Richard Posner has commented that the reason lawyers find analogical arguments "irresistible" is that they enable lawyers "to reach conclusions without reading much beyond what is in law books," and he

---

* Edward H. Levi, *An Introduction to Legal Reasoning* 3 and n.5 (1949). "The logical fallacy is the fallacy of the undistributed middle or the fallacy of assuming the antecedent is true because the consequence has been affirmed." Id. at n.5. Levi referred to analogical reasoning as "reasoning by example" or "reasoning from case to case." Id. at 1.

suggests that judges' reliance on them similarly reflects an unwillingness to look outside their chambers.[8] "It is no surprise," he says, "that 'real' reasoning by analogy – going from an old to a new case on the basis of some felt 'similarity' – has been a source of many pernicious judicial doctrines."[*]

The most common assessment of analogical arguments in the law goes beyond praise or blame and asserts bluntly that there is no such thing. There can be no reasoning "by example" from one concrete instance to another, it is said, except by way of a general principle that subsumes them both. So, if someone observes that Socrates is a man and is mortal and reasons that Alcibiades, being a man, is, by analogy with Socrates, also mortal, she really reasons that since all men are mortal and Alcibiades is a man, Alcibiades is mortal. If not, she does not, properly speaking, *reason* at all; if her conclusion is correct, it is only by happenstance. Without some general statement that relevantly associates Socrates and Alcibiades, there is no basis, analogical or otherwise, to ascribe the mortality

---

[*] Richard Posner, *Overcoming Law* 519 (1995). Posner says that he does not "wish to bad-mouth analogy," id., and he has use for it in a number of ways. See id. at 518–522; Richard A. Posner, *The Problems of Jurisprudence* 86–92 (1990). But the praise is faint. "[R]easoning by analogy," he says, has "no definite content or integrity; it denotes an unstable class of disparate reasoning methods." Id. at 86. Observing that "[t]he heart of legal reasoning as conceived by most modern lawyers is reasoning by analogy," id., he says, "I merely question whether reasoning by analogy, when distinguished from logical deduction and scientific induction on the one hand and stare decisis on the other, deserves the hoopla and reverence that members of the legal profession have bestowed on it." Id. at 90.

of the former to the latter. So-called analogical argument, Larry Alexander concludes, is a "phantasm"; "it does not really exist."*

For all the differences among these views, there is broad agreement that, possibly benign political effects aside, the law could and would do better not to rely on analogical arguments – "logically flawed," "pernicious," a "phantasm" – at all. This agreement is the more remarkable because, despite their own insistent attention to the reasoning that supports a legal outcome, lawyers and judges seem entirely unaware of any such problem. If, as Posner says, lawyers find analogical arguments irresistible in their own work, it is hard to understand why they are unable to resist them in the briefs of opposing

---

* Larry Alexander, *Bad Beginnings*, 145 U. Pa. L. Rev. 57, 86 (1996). For similar views, without the name-calling, see, e.g., Melvin Aron Eisenberg, *The Nature of the Common Law* 83 (1988) ("Reasoning by analogy differs from reasoning from precedent and principle only in form"); Kent Greenawalt, *Law and Objectivity* 200 (1992) ("[R]easoning by analogy is not sharply divided from reasoning in terms of general propositions"); Neil MacCormick, *Legal Reasoning and Legal Theory* 161, 186 (1978) ("[N]o clear line can be drawn between arguments from principle and from analogy," "Analogies only make sense if there are reasons of principle underlying them"); Peter Westen, *On "Confusing Ideas": Reply*, 91 Yale L.J. 1153, 1163 (1982) ("One can never declare A to be legally similar to B without first formulating the legal rule of treatment by which they are rendered relevantly identical"). Dworkin's "vertical and horizontal ordering" of legal reasoning, see p. 7, also belongs in this camp. He has observed: "[A]nalogy without theory is blind. An analogy is a way of stating a conclusion, not a way of reaching one, and theory must do the real work." Dworkin, *In Praise of Theory*, 29 Ariz. St. L.J. 353, 371 (1997). Cass Sunstein appears to agree in principle – "[A]nalogical reasoning cannot proceed without identification of a governing idea" – but he believes that in practice, analogical reasoning helps to identify the idea rather than the other way around. Cass Sunstein, *Legal Reasoning and Political Conflict* 65 (1996). See p. 31.

counsel. Although particular analogies are often at the center of contention between lawyers on opposite sides and between majority and dissenting judges, there is scarcely a trace of criticism of analogical argument generally. On the contrary, the importance that is usually attached to the choice of analogy suggests quite the opposite. Not only do analogical arguments figure prominently in briefs and opinions. They are also a standard feature, one might almost say defining feature, of legal education.*

The view of legal reasoning that excludes the use of analogy, except, perhaps, on sufferance as a kind of useful ineptitude, or regards it as an elliptical deductive argument is mistaken. Analogical legal arguments differ from the analogical arguments that we make routinely in everyday life only in their subject matter. In law as in life, analogical argument is a valid, albeit undemonstrable, form of reasoning that stands on its own and has its own credentials, which are not derived from abstract reason but are rooted in the experience and knowledge of the lawyers and judges who employ it. Some analogical arguments are good and some are bad. Ordinarily, we know how to tell one from the other and are able to reach a fair degree of agreement about which is which. The human capacity for reasoning by analogy presents complex and difficult

* See pp. 142–146.

epistemological questions, but its use is commonplace and, carefully used, its conclusions are generally reliable.

The prominence of analogical arguments in legal reasoning is not accidental. It is in the nature of law to be a matter of rules, the principled application of which to concrete cases is accomplished by analogical reasoning. That is contrary to the model of legal reasoning as fully contained within a hierarchy of rules connected inferentially and to the rejection of analogical reasoning as arbitrary and subversive of the rule of law.* Without the intervention of analogical arguments, legal rules and the rule of law itself would be only theoretical constructs.

These are large claims, which are explained and defended in the chapters that follow.

On its face, the contrast between the scholarly critique of analogical reasoning and its pervasive use and acceptance in practice is puzzling. It suggests that the impulse behind efforts to measure legal reasoning by the rules of formal logic and methods of empirical science is not prompted by a weakness in the arguments themselves. Rather, it springs more deeply from a conviction that it is not enough for law to be reasonable, as an accommodation of the interests of individuals living together in community, and that law must be independent of the contingencies of human experience and anchored wholly

---

* On the rule of law, see pp. 147–152.

[13]

and absolutely in reason. Although those who criticize the use of analogical arguments do not generally make the connection, one can detect in their criticism the same concern for the validity of law that fuels the perennial jurisprudential debate between natural law and legal positivism, which the horrors of Nazism made urgent after World War II[9] and which, more recently, has sparked debate about the canons of constitutionalism and legal interpretation.[10] (Cass Sunstein has observed that Levi's effort to tie the use of analogy in the law to democracy was a response to the Legal Realists' attack on legal reasoning as "political" and undemocratic.[11]) The immediate focus of the methodological issue and the substantive one are different, the former having to do specifically with the process of adjudication and the latter with law at large. But both issues are responsive to the perception of a gap between the law's great normative force, on one hand, and its supposed lack of rational force, on the other. From that perspective, the debate about analogical reasoning in the law concerns more than a logician's nicety or a professional trope. It belongs within the long history of debate whether the law is a product of reason or of will, whether in the end the law is the law because it is right or only because of the power of those who proclaim it. So understood, the use of analogy in legal reasoning is worth studying, not just as an important feature of the lawyer's craft but because it is a critical locus of the law's normative claims and brings us closer to an understanding of law itself.

Because analogical argument is so familiar a part of the legal landscape and, scholarly criticism aside, so unquestioned, it is worthwhile to set forth the case against it, before coming to its defense. In Chapter 1, I discuss Scott Brewer's account of analogical legal reasoning at some length.[12] Brewer's analysis is the most complete and broad-ranging, and, in one way or another, it incorporates all the issues that have been raised elsewhere. Although he characterizes his analysis as an approving account, it highlights the generally disapproving positions with which I disagree. The difficulties of Brewer's account that are discussed here prefigure the objections to analogical legal reasoning that are discussed at length in Chapter 3. Chapter 2 provides three cases or sets of cases for discussion. One, *Adams v. New Jersey Steamboat Co.*,[13] is drawn from the common law and has figured in other discussions of the use of analogy in law.[14] The second is a set of four cases decided by the Supreme Court over a forty-four-year period, in which the Court construed provisions of the federal Copyright Act that had to do with radio and television broadcast transmissions.[15] Third are two cases, *Olmstead v. United States*[16] and *Katz v. United States*,[17] in which, with a thirty-nine-year gap in between, the Supreme Court considered a question of constitutional law arising under the Fourth Amendment.* Together, the cases display clearly the courts' reliance on analogical reasoning. Far from being uncomfortable or uneasy about it, they rely on analogical reasoning confidently, not as a makeshift, best-we-can-do substitute for something else, but as a central part of the argument being made.

Chapters 3 and 4 are the heart of the book. Chapter 3 begins with a reminder of how pervasively analogical reasoning is used in everyday life. It then draws on the examples developed in Chapter 2 to describe the place of analogical reasoning in the arguments of lawyers and judges. Discussing the process of adjudication generally, it explains why, in the nature of law, analogical reasoning is not merely useful but is indispensable. Finally, the chapter addresses arguments that analogical reasoning, on its own terms, is defective and too weak to bear the weight placed on it.

In Chapter 4, I discuss briefly how it is that, assertions to the contrary notwithstanding, we are able to make arguments by analogy and to have confidence in the outcomes. That is followed by a discussion of the "case method" of legal education, in which analogical reasoning plays a central role. The chapter

* The choice of these three examples has no special significance. *Adams*, as noted, has been used as an example by others in their discussions of analogy. The choice of the other two examples is explained by the fact that I regularly teach copyright and constitutional criminal procedure.

continues with a discussion of how analogical reasoning is related to the rule of law. In the concluding pages, I make the connection between the search for certainty in legal reasoning and the search for objective validity in the law itself. In both cases, the search springs plausibly from the same source, a felt need to vindicate incontrovertibly the law's normative claims. Such certitude is not to be found. Rather, the law is sustained by the conscientious application of human reason and good will.

CHAPTER ONE

Analogy and Inductive
and Deductive Reasoning

Scott Brewer's account of analogical legal arguments includes them within a broad family of legal and nonlegal arguments, characterized by "the use of examples in the process of moving from premises to conclusion."[1] Among the other kinds of legal argument within this family, he mentions reasoning from precedents, application of "equal protection" norms, and the "*ejusdem generis*" canon for the construction of documents.*

---

* Scott Brewer, *Exemplary Reasoning: Semantics, Pragmatics, and the Rational Force of Legal Argument by Analogy*, 109 Harv. L. Rev. 923, 934–938 (1996). The "*ejusdem generis*" rule is that a term in a series should be construed consistently with other more specific terms in the same series. For example, in *Tallmadge v. Stevenson*, 681 N.E.2d 476 (Ohio App. 1996), construing an ordinance providing that "no person being the owner or having charge of cattle, horses, swine, sheep, geese, ducks, goats, turkeys, chickens or other fowl or animals shall permit them to run at large," the court said that a cat is not included among "other animals." Under the doctrine of *ejusdem generis*, the court said, that phrase included only other farm animals, like those enumerated, and although cats may be found on farms, they are not considered to be farm animals but are household pets.

An analogical argument, he says, consists of more than the analogy itself. It is a patterned series of steps, the "rational force" of which depends on "the relation between the truth of the argument's premises and that of its conclusion."[2] His principal concern is to show that the employment of an analogy in the manner he describes gives the resulting argument a good deal more rational force than is generally supposed.

The pattern of analogical argument, Brewer says, includes three steps:

1. Abduction in a context of doubt.[3] The reasoner is uncertain about the extension of some term – what it refers to – that has legal consequences in the case under consideration. More concretely, he is uncertain about how legally to classify some phenomenon – person, thing, event, or circumstance – with respect to the matter in question. So, for example, he may be uncertain whether it is a *search* to which the Fourth Amendment applies if a trained dog sniffs closed luggage left in a public place and signals to the police that it contains drugs.[4] If it is a search, then, unless requirements of the Amendment have been met, information obtained as a result of the sniff is not admissible in evidence against the owner of the luggage, because the sniff violated his constitutional rights. If the sniff is not a search, the Amendment is not applicable, and the information is constitutionally admissible. Noting some examples of police conduct that are more or less similar, and relating the dog-sniff (the *target*) by analogy to one or more of them (the *source*), the reasoner *abduces* a rule that appears acceptably to sort the target and the source into conduct that is and conduct that is not a search and thereby determines whether the sniff is a search.

Brewer treats abduction, which is not generally a familiar concept, as a form of inference, like deduction and induction, in which there is a particular relation between the truth of the premises and the truth of the conclusion. Just as the truth of the premises of a valid deductive argument guarantees the truth of the conclusion and the truth of the premises of a valid inductive argument makes the truth of the conclusion probable, the truth of the premises of an abductive argument makes the truth of the conclusion possible. So, for example, noticing that the front lawn is wet and observing that the lawn would be wet if it had rained during the night, one might abduce the conclusion that it had rained. It is true, of course, that the lawn would be wet also if a neighbor's children had staged a water fight on the lawn during the night, or if the fire department had tested its hoses on the lawn, or if a water main in the street had broken, or if a stream underground had burst forth, or if Neptune had held court on the lawn, or any number of other possibilities. So far as the *logical form* of the argument is concerned, any of those conclusions is as likely as the conclusion that it had rained.* Abduction establishes only that it is *possible* that it had rained; for if the lawn were not wet, then (in the absence of other special circumstances) it would not be possible that it had rained. Abduction is, therefore, a very weak form of inference, if, indeed, it is properly regarded as an inference at all.†

Brewer's account of abduction as the first step in a legal argument by analogy is derived from Charles Peirce's account of scientific discovery.[5] According to Peirce, when a scientific

---

* The best-known examples of abductive inference are the "deductions" of Sherlock Holmes. Holmes regularly makes elaborate inferences from a few small observations. The possibility that there are other, equally plausible ways to account for his observations is mostly ignored. See Umberto Eco and Thomas A. Sebeok, eds., *The Sign of Three* (1983).

† Brewer notes that there is disagreement whether abduction is properly regarded as subject to "rational constraint," Brewer, p. 19n., at 946, by which I take him to mean that it has a definite logical form that justifies an inference from premises to conclusion. He affirms somewhat equivocally his belief that abduction is subject to rational constraint, that it is "a disciplined (albeit . . . not a rigidly guided) form of inference . . . [and] has a substantial degree of rational force." Id. at 947. I see no reason to dissent from that, provided that one is aware of just how weak an inference it is. So far as logical form is concerned, the inference from the premise, "the lawn is wet," to the conclusion, "it rained last night," is simply invalid, unless one qualifies the conclusion with the words "might have." Still, a weak inference is better than no inference at all. It at least rejects a conclusion (derivable from the premises (1) that if it rains at night the lawn is wet the next morning, and (2) that the lawn is not wet) that it did *not* rain last night. Nevertheless, since there are, so far as logical form is concerned, any number of valid abductive inferences from a premise, it will not do to put much weight on the logical force of abduction. The interesting question is how one abduces to the *correct* conclusion, which Brewer's account does not address, because the abductive inference is superseded by inductive and deductive inferences in the completed argument and has no bearing on the conclusion. See pp. 33–38.

researcher notes an unfamiliar natural phenomenon and seeks to explain it, he typically hypothesizes an explanation out of all the theoretically possible explanations. His choice of hypothesis is not validated deductively or inductively; nevertheless, unless the choice had some valid basis, the task of formulating and testing hypotheses would be endless, and discovery of the correct explanation would be a matter of luck. There is disagreement among philosophers of science whether the process of scientific discovery has any moorings in reason or is rather a phenomenon to be explained wholly psychologically.[6] It is evident, at any rate, that abducing a hypothesis need not be a random procedure. For someone with knowledge of the field to which the phenomenon belongs is far more likely to hit on the correct hypothesis than someone who knows nothing about it. The hypothesis that it rained last night is presumably the one most likely to be correct. But suppose the question were put to a creature newly arrived from Mars, who knew nothing about earthly matters. How would "he" come up with an answer? Or suppose one knew that the neighbor's children were always having water fights on the lawn. Asked to abduce an explanation for the wet lawn, the visitor from Mars would be utterly at a loss, unless, at least, he supposed that conditions on Earth resembled those back home. The person who knew about the aqueous habits of the neighbor's children, on the other hand, would have no difficulty.

So, Brewer avers, confronted by the drug-sniffing dog (or its police handler), a judge may take note of rules indicated by prior cases: if a police officer in a public place sees something in plain view, it is not a search for purposes of the Fourth Amendment, whereas if he opens luggage and observes something plainly visible inside, it is a search; if he overhears a conversation in a public place, it is not a search, but if he listens surreptitiously to a conversation in a private place, it is a search; and so forth. Considering these and other rules, the judge abduces a rule that resolves the case before her: If a police officer obtains information about a person or thing in a public place without intrusion on the person or taking possession of or interfering with the use of the thing, it is not a search for purposes of the Fourth Amendment. Brewer calls this abduced rule an "analogy-warranting rule" or AWR.[7] It is analogy-warranting because it contains in the generalized form of a rule the analogical connection between the source and the target that inspired it. So in this instance, the judge notices the similarity between observing or overhearing a person in a public place (the source) and a dog sniffing a container in a public place (the target), and she concludes by analogy that since the former is not a search under the Fourth Amendment, the latter also is not. The AWR provides a generalization from which a conclusion about the facts of the particular case – dog sniffing suitcase – can be deduced.*

2. Confirmation or disconfirmation of the AWR.[8] The AWR as initially abduced is only preliminary. Just as the scientist subjects his hypothesis to experiments that confirm or disconfirm it inductively, the legal reasoner tests the AWR by considering whether its application acceptably classifies the target phenomenon and other related phenomena, those that he had in mind when formulating the AWR and others. He entertains arguments of policy and efficiency that explain and justify the AWR or, on the other hand, contradict it. So, in the case of the sniffing dog, justificatory arguments might include:

---

* Although the rule as stated is sufficient to resolve the case at hand deductively, it is evident that it may have to be refined in another case with different facts. Suppose a police officer were to use an X-ray machine that allowed him to see what is inside a container without opening it or taking possession of it. By its terms the rule is applicable. But, confronting the new facts, one may want to amend it by adding "and without using a technological device." Or one may not. See *Kyllo v. United States*, 533 U.S. 27 (2001). There are differences between the process of abduction that Peirce described and the process of analogical reasoning that concerns Brewer. The abduced scientific hypothesis is descriptive; it explains the observed phenomenon (the wet lawn). The abduced legal rule is prescriptive; it prescribes a legal outcome with respect to the phenomenon in question (dog sniffing luggage). The difference, which may be significant for other purposes, does not affect Brewer's basic point, which is that the function of an analogy in legal reasoning is only to prompt the reasoning that validates a decision, as the abduced scientific hypothesis prompts the experimentation that confirms (or disconfirms) the explanation. As the subsequent steps of Brewer's process make plain, the analogy plays no part in the validation itself. In this way, Brewer explains the prominence of analogies in legal reasoning without having to recognize analogy as a distinct form of reasoning.

a sniffing dog signals the presence of nothing except drugs, so there is no significant invasion of privacy; if a container does not contain drugs, its owner will not even be aware that it has been sniffed; trained dogs are an effective, inexpensive, and unintrusive way to control the transportation of drugs. Arguments that contradict the AWR might include: What a person deliberately conceals from view should not ordinarily be subject to exposure without his consent; persons should not have to be on guard against unusual and undetectable methods of investigation; the lawfulness of an investigative tactic should not depend on what, if anything, it turns up. Brewer calls these arguments "analogy-warranting rationales" or AWRas.[9] Working back and forth with the phenomenon in question, other examples of similar phenomena, and relevant legal doctrine, the reasoner reconsiders the AWR and the AWRas and, by a process of reciprocal "'reflective adjustment,'"[10] arrives at a rule that acceptably classifies the phenomenon with respect to the issue before him: *If a dog is made to sniff luggage, without interfering with it or its owner, for the purpose of revealing whether it contains drugs, there is not a search to which the requirements of the Fourth Amendment apply.* The rule must be consistent with other valid rules of law (which may themselves have had to be modified) and lead deductively to a conclusion when applied to the facts of the case before the court. Brewer continues to call this modified rule an "AWR," although the analogy, having prompted abduction to the initial AWR, has no further role to play and is discarded.

3. Application of the AWR.[11] Having formulated a rule covering the phenomenon that provoked his inquiry, the reasoner applies it and, by a valid deductive inference, reaches the appropriate conclusion.

Although Brewer refers to the whole three-step process as an analogical argument, it is apparent that the work of the analogy is completed in the first step. True to Brewer's observation that abduction from an analogy to a rule (AWR) that explains it is an invalid inference,[12] the significance of the analogy is in his view not logical, not justificatory at all, but epistemological or psychological; it explains how the lawyer or judge happened to hit on that particular rule out of all the possible rules.* But, having set the reasoner on the right track, the analogy has no more to do; it helps him neither to reach his destination nor even to determine whether he has in fact reached it.† Once the analogy has prompted the formulation of an AWR, it drops from sight and need never be mentioned again or, indeed, even be known; for aught that appears, the

---

* Inasmuch as the abduction from the analogy to the AWR is unexplained, see p. 32, even this information is significantly limited.
† Posner evidently agrees. Analogy, he says, belongs to the "logic of discovery," not the logic of "justification." Richard A. Posner, *The Problems of Jurisprudence* 91 (1990).

AWR might just as easily have been found in a dream* or, as sometimes is said, have "popped" into the reasoner's head. Both elements of the analogy, the source and the target, may reappear in the second, confirmatory stage, but only as examples, among others, by which to test the AWR. The relationship between AWR and AWRa is established by ordinary arguments of policy and efficiency, on one hand, and consistency, on the other. The third step of the process, application of the confirmed AWR to the particular facts, is, as Brewer insists, deductive. Looking back on the argument from the end to the beginning, one does not encounter the analogy as such at all, for it has no place in the argument's logical structure. What is offered as an account and defense of analogical argument in legal reasoning turns out to assign it only an incidental and dispensable, if common and often useful, role. All the work that counts, the work of justification, is done in the second step, by the AWRa.

It is apparent that Brewer is led to embed an analogy in this three-step process because he believes that, standing on its own, it has no rational force. An analogy, he explains, consists of an observed similarity between two phenomena, the source and the target, identification by observation or otherwise of some further characteristic of the source, and the conclusion

---

* Talking about the process of scientific discovery, Brewer suggests that a dream might serve in place of an analogy. Brewer, p. 19n., at 979.

that the target (probably) also has that characteristic.[13] The logical form of an analogy is thus:

(1) A (the source) has characteristics p, q, and r;

(2) B (the target) has characteristics p, q, and r;

(3) A has also characteristic s;

(4) Therefore, B has characteristic s.

But propositions (1)–(3) do not sustain (4), without an additional premise:

(3^1) If anything that has characteristics p, q, and r has characteristic s, then everything that has characteristics p, q, and r has characteristic s.

With the addition of (3^1), it is possible to construct a valid syllogism. More simply stated:

(3^2) Anything that has characteristics p, q, and r has characteristic s;

(2) B has characteristics p, q, and r;

(4) Therefore B has characteristic s.

A straightforward analogy, embracing neither a proposition of the form (3^1) nor a proposition of the form (3^2), is simply invalid. From the logical, or analytic, point of view, there is no more to be said. Brewer overcomes this invalidity by associating the analogy with the inductive second step and the deductive third step; but they do not buttress the analogy so much as ignore it. If, as he says, the completed argument depends on the relation between premises and conclusion, its rational force is no greater with the analogy than without it. Thus, despite his approving stance, Brewer seems at one with a group to whom he refers as "skeptics," who reject analogical reasoning altogether.[14]

Brewer contrasts the skeptics with those who have more confidence in the persuasive force of an analogy, whom he calls "mystics."[15] Levi, who endorsed analogical reasoning without explaining it, was presumably a mystic. Among recent scholars, the mystic-in-chief, Brewer says, is Cass Sunstein,[16] who has generally followed Levi's lead. Like Levi, Sunstein observes that "reasoning by analogy...is the mode through which the ordinary lawyer operates,"[17] and he commends it as a means of resolving disputes when there is not agreement about underlying principles. Lawyers and judges resort to analogical reasoning, he says, when they lack a "comprehensive theory that would account for the particular outcomes [analogical reasoning] yields."[18] Such reasoning, Sunstein says, gives rise to "[i]ncompletely theorized agreements," which permit resolution of concrete disputes despite more fundamental incertitude or disagreement.[19] Whereas Levi had found democratic virtues in such outcomes, because "the examples or analogies urged by the parties bring into the law the common ideas of the society,"[20] Sunstein sees no special connection with democracy. It would be "most surprising," he observes, "if we could identify any mechanism translating democratic wishes into analogical reasoning.... The force of any argument by analogy really turns on underlying principles and not on community desires."[21] Nevertheless, he commends the use of analogy, because it frequently allows a heterogeneous and even deeply divided community to achieve a limited consensus that preserves the rule of law.

Brewer gently derides the mystics as believing that an analogy "has some ineffable quality that merits our entrusting it with deep and difficult matters of state."[22] His point is well taken. For Levi acknowledges explicitly that analogical reasoning is logically flawed, and Sunstein, in effect, does as well. Extolling the virtues of incompletely theorized agreements reached on the basis of an analogy, Sunstein says in an aside: "To be sure, analogical reasoning cannot proceed without identification of a governing idea... to account for the results in the source and target cases."[23] The analogy is important nevertheless, he says, because it "helps identify the governing idea."[24] That, however, has no more to do with the validity of the argument than Brewer's abductive step does. From a logical point of view, the crux of the matter is that analogical reasoning "cannot proceed" on its own. Taking his words at face value, Sunstein is a skeptic in mystic's clothing.

And, indeed, why ought we credit Levi's or Sunstein's benign view of analogical arguments? If, as they say, analogical arguments are bad arguments, why should we count on them regularly to produce good results? Either Levi and Sunstein must be mistaken about the formal weakness of the arguments or, one supposes, they must be mistaken about their merits.

Brewer himself has remarkably little to say about an analogy, beyond pointing out its deductive invalidity.[25] He does say that "there is inevitably an uncodifiable, imaginative moment in exemplary, analogical reasoning," and that "[t]here is an art to making apt, instructive, compelling analogies."[26] This "uncodifiable, imaginative moment" or "art" is what the mystics might label simply as "intuition." Brewer avoids his own criticism of the mystics only by arguing, in effect, that whatever may be the ground or origin of an analogy, it has no formal place in a proper legal argument anyway, and, therefore, does not affect the argument's rational force.

The heart of the matter, Brewer asserts, and the reason why analogies are so hard to tame, is the requirement of *relevant similarity*.[27] All accounts of analogical argument agree that an analogy is successful and justifies its conclusion only if the observed similarity between the source and the target is relevant to the further similarity that is in question.* The

---

* Although it may be said loosely that whether an analogy is good or bad depends simply on the extent or strength of the similarity between the two items – source

point is obvious. No one, except a small child, would expect a red tennis ball to taste like an apple, although they are considerably similar in size, shape, and color; those similarities, strong enough in some respects, are not relevant to how they taste. But, Brewer says, the notion of relevant similarity is "tenaciously resistant to conceptual explication" and leaves the logical force of analogical arguments "largely mysterious and unanalyzed."[28] The second step of his process, confirmation of the AWR, might be regarded as an effort to unpack the notion of relevant similarity, without a commitment to the epistemic priority of either the observed similarity or the factors that make it relevant. So, one might say, a source and target are relevantly similar and the analogy is successful if there are reasons (AWRas) to conclude that the characteristics that are observed to be similar are regularly accompanied by the characteristic that is in doubt. But Brewer intends more – and less – than that. He wants to account for the prominence of analogies in legal reasoning and, therefore, to give them an effective place in legal arguments; hence the role of analogy in the first step, abduction to the AWR. In the end, however, his interest is not epistemological but logical, not the psychological or intellectual origins of a legal argument

and target – being compared, the difference is a matter not of quantity or strength but of relevance. Two items that closely resemble one another might nevertheless compose a bad analogy, because they are dissimilar in some respect that is highly relevant to the matter at hand but is otherwise insignificant.

but its power rationally to persuade. Consequently, denying an analogy any rational force of its own, Brewer has no analytic use for it and discards it in the completed argument. Even if judges and lawyers give independent weight to an analogy and do not construct their arguments according to his model, he says, we should reconstruct them in that fashion in order to display their rational force. The reconstruction avoids the invalid abductive inference from conclusion to premise, or consequence to antecedent, by replacing it with a convincing inductively validated instrumental argument (the AWRa) for a proposition (the confirmed AWR) from which a conclusion about the case at hand can be formally deduced. The confirmed AWR is, in effect, the major premise and the facts of the case the minor premise of a valid syllogism.

Brewer believes that his account of analogical argument in legal reasoning sustains our aspiration to the rule of law.[29] Just what the rule of law signifies concretely is far from clear; aspirationally, it is closely allied with the view of law as reason, not subject to individual will or whim but rather conforming to rational criteria.* According to that view, a concrete legal problem is to be solved not by considering it in all its concrete particularity and devising an equally particular solution, but by finding or formulating a rule that has hitherto,

* See pp. 150–160.

actually or in contemplation, been applied to problems of that kind and will thereafter, actually or in contemplation, also be so applied. Making a place for the AWR, which is itself brought into reflective adjustment with other legal rules by the AWRa, appears to satisfy this feature of law, and the deductive form of the eventual argument carries it out with the full vigor of formal logic.[30] It is not an accident, however, that the third step of the argument omits entirely not only the analogy with which the argument began but also, and for this purpose more significantly, the AWRa. Since the whole point of the second step is to fashion an AWR that applies specifically to the particular facts of the case, application of the AWR in the third step is no more than confirmation of a conclusion that has already effectively been reached.* In its final form, the argument achieves formal validity at the price of being an empty shell.

In the fully expanded argument, on the other hand, the AWRa is prominently included, but only at the price of undermining the rule of law. The initial abduction of the AWR in the first step is not sufficient to sustain the claim of reason;

---

* There is no guarantee that the AWR in its final form will be applied in any subsequent case. For it will simply be one among other rules and policies considered as part of the AWRa leading to formulation of a confirmed AWR for that case. Nor is there even a guarantee that it will retain just the same form as an element of the AWRa in a subsequent case. For it will be up to the court in that case to extract the rule of prior cases for use in the case at hand. See pp. 98–99.

nor could it be, because, as Brewer insists, an abductive inference is formally invalid. It has to be confirmed by reference
to the AWRa, which explains and justifies it.[31] Yet it is precisely the point of the rule of law and the whole function of
the AWR in Brewer's account that a rule ordinarily be applied
because it is the rule and not because it is independently justified.* To be sure, a rule may be called into question and, if
it is, reasons for following it will be demanded. Even then,
however, adherence to the rule of law and a proper respect
for the difference between legislation and adjudication dictate that the reasons be sought within the fabric of the law
and not in the open spaces of policy and its efficient imple-
mentation. Choosing or framing one rule rather than another
may call for intelligent consideration of the legal landscape
being mapped. But that is another matter from subjecting
the rule of a case to confirmation or disconfirmation in every instance, by explanatory and justificatory reasons at large.
Brewer may respond that he does not require a full-blown inquiry into the AWRa in every instance; if the posited AWR is
well-known and uncontested, it may be accepted on that basis.
The question, however, is not whether we may not sometimes

---

* Frederick Schauer has written illuminatingly on the difference between following
  a rule because it is the rule and acting according to the rule because that is, all
  things considered, the sensible way to act. Frederick Schauer, *Playing by the
  Rules* 112–134 (1991). Brewer's account of analogical reasoning regards the rule
  of decision (AWR) in a case as subject to revision on the basis of the AWRa.

take a shortcut but whether in principle we want to go that route at all. Wanting to steer a middle course between the formalists who claim for the law the validity of a deductive system and those who, rejecting formalism, charge that the law is subject to no principled restraint, Brewer has given us some of the difficulties of both. The formalist's claim is sustained, but the deductive system on which he relies is empty. And the antiformalist is released from even the restraint of adherence to a rule, because he is invited in every instance to subject the rule on which he relies to the test of instrumental justification.

Seeking to domesticate analogical legal arguments and bring them within the ambit of inferential logic, Brewer does not, as he believes, sustain the rule of law but defeats it. For no self-contained body of rules, however they are determined and however they may be related to one another, can prescribe fully the rules' application to the specific facts of a concrete case.* Rules simply as rules remain inevitably general. Without the tether that analogical arguments provide, the rule of law would be an abstract ideal cut off from the decision of actual cases.

In sum, purporting to explain the prominence of analogical arguments in legal reasoning, Brewer relegates the analogy

---

* See pp. 88–91.

itself to an insignificant role. Because he believes that an analogy on its own terms rests on an invalid inference and has no rational force, he assigns it merely the incidental function of setting his three-step sequence of abduction, induction, and deduction in motion. One may well wonder why the completed sequence is called an "analogical" argument at all, if not to account, however superficially, for the fact that the use of analogy is a distinguishing characteristic of legal reasoning. At the same time, depriving the analogy of any independent significance, his account of legal reasoning contains no means by which rules are made to apply to concrete cases as rules and not simply as the best course to follow, all things considered. When all is said and done, he leaves unexplained the puzzle of lawyers' and judges' reliance on analogical reasoning, on the one hand, and its widespread disparagement and rejection by legal scholars, on the other.

Brewer's defense of the rational force of analogical legal argument, reconstructed as he prescribes, is, at bottom, an effort to vindicate law as reason rather than will, in the tradition of theories of natural law, according to which the validity of law depends on its conformity to some external standard of truth and not simply the authority of those who promulgate it. If, the defense goes, analogical arguments in the law can, despite appearances, be subjected to the demands of reason, then

fidelity to law may be warranted.* The reconstruction does not succeed, because it has the effect not of validating analogical arguments but of making them irrelevant. Their place in legal reasoning is too insistent for that. The use of analogy is, as everyone agrees, not occasional or incidental but pervasive, and on its face its use is to persuade; it is not merely an interesting aside or the report of a psychological event. Nor can it be dismissed as only a curious habit of the legal profession – what the French call a *déformation professionelle* – or simply a mistake. If the normative force of law depends on its commitment to reason, a place has to be found for analogical arguments on their own terms.

---

* One may object that, whatever the rational force of the reconstructed argument, the uneliminable normative element of the AWRa leaves law ultimately a product of will. Brewer does not address that question. I think he would say that unless the argumentation of legal reasoning is valid, it hardly matters what footing there is for the law's normative stance; if his rescue of the rational force of legal argument is not sufficient to dispose of the broader issue, nevertheless, it is necessary. His evident passionate concern for the rationality of law makes it most unlikely that he would give it all up as a bad job anyway. For myself, the assertion that the inability to *demonstrate* the ultimate normative ground of law – its dependence on a basic norm, see Hans Kelsen, *Pure Theory of Law* 46 (trans. from the Second German ed., M. Knight, trans., 1967) or "rule of recognition," see H.L.A. Hart, *The Concept of Law* 94–95 (2d ed. 1994) – means that it is (ultimately) a product not of reason but of will unduly restricts the bounds of reason, the mistake that I believe Brewer makes with respect to legal argumentation. See pp. 150–152.

Steamboats, Broadcast Transmissions, and Electronic Eavesdropping

a. Common law: *Adams v. New Jersey Steamboat Co.*

Adams was a passenger on the defendant's steamboat, going from New York to Albany. During the night, having locked the door and fastened the windows of his stateroom, he left a sum of money in his clothing. The money was stolen by someone who apparently managed to reach through one of the windows. Adams sued to recover the amount of his loss. The jury returned a verdict for Adams, and judgment was entered in his favor. On appeal, the judgment was affirmed, and the defendant took a further appeal to the New York Court of Appeals.[1]

The only question before the court was whether the trial court had properly instructed the jury that, in the circumstances, the defendant was liable as an insurer, without proof that it had been negligent. In its opinion, having stated the issue, the court turned without further elaboration to the rule that innkeepers were liable as insurers for the losses of their guests. The rule, the court said, was based on public policy: innkeepers should have a "high degree of responsibility" because of the "extraordinary confidence... necessarily reposed in them" and the "great temptation to fraud and danger of plunder" created by "the peculiar relations of the parties."[2] The relations of a steamboat operator to its passengers, the court went on, "differ in no essential respect": "[t]he passenger procures and pays for his room for the same reasons that a guest at an inn does," and "[t]here are the same opportunities for fraud and plunder" that tempt an innkeeper.[3] Indeed, "[a] steamer carrying passengers upon the water, and furnishing them with rooms and entertainment, is, for all practical purposes, a floating inn."[4] "[S]ince the same considerations of public policy apply to both relations," the rule in the two cases should be the same.[5] One might have thought that the stateroom of a steamboat resembles a berth in the sleeping car of a railroad, the operator of which did not have an insurer's liability, more than it does a room at an inn, since both of the former involve travel from one place to another. But the court thought otherwise and added a lengthy passage that distinguished the relations between a steamboat operator and

its passengers from those between an operator of a railroad sleeping car and its passengers.[6] The court then returned to the main theme. A steamboat is one of those "modern floating palaces,"[7] and a traveler on a steamboat "establishes legal relations with the carrier that cannot well be distinguished from those that exist between the hotelkeeper and his guests. . . . The two relations, if not identical, bear such close analogy to each other that the same rule of responsibility should govern."[8]

The analogy between an inn and a steamboat that provides staterooms for passengers evidently plays a large role in the court's reasoning. Arguments of public policy are deployed to explain the existing rule applicable to inns, which is then applied to steamboats on the basis of the analogy. Likewise, the court is at pains to explain why there is not a relevant analogy between a railroad sleeping car and an inn.[9] It adds a reason of policy: "[T]he passenger has no right to expect, and in fact does not expect, the same degree of security from thieves while in an open berth in a car on a railroad as in a stateroom of a steamboat, securely locked and otherwise guarded from intrusion."[10] Even that, however, is supported by the analogy between the stateroom and a room at an inn.*

---

* "In the latter case [a passenger in a stateroom], when he retires for the night, he ought to be able to rely upon the company for his protection *with the same faith that the guest can rely upon the protection of the innkeeper, since the two relations are quite analogous.* In the former [a passenger in a sleeping car] the contract and the relations of the parties differ at least to such an extent as to justify some

The significance of the analogy between an inn and a steamboat is brought out if one compares the court's argument as it reads with Brewer's reconstruction of it, which hardly makes a polite bow to the analogy between an inn and a steamboat before dismissing it.[11] The role of the analogy, he says, is to lead the court by abduction to a general rule (AWR) that if a person reposes great confidence in another, in circumstances that create a great temptation to fraud and danger of plunder, the latter is liable as an insurer for the former's loss. The analogy bears no rational weight of its own and does not of itself give any support to the rule. That the court hit on that analogy is itself not explained; it is, evidently, simply an "uncodifiable, imaginative moment."* The rule is then tested and supported by consideration of the policies favoring such liability (the AWRa) and by comparing it to alternative rules that apply in other circumstances.[12]

It is not difficult to reconstruct the court's argument as Brewer proposes. But the reconstruction transforms the argument. It radically diminishes the role actually played by the analogy, which does not function merely as a stimulus to the court's reasoning but rather is central to it, and it imports

---

modification of the common law rule of responsibility [i.e., the rule applicable to innkeepers]." *Adams v. New Jersey Steamboat Co.,* 151 N.Y. 163, 169 (1896) (emphasis added).

* See p. 32.

into the opinion a general rule far broader than anything that the court says. One might infer from the opinion that at least in some circumstances, if confidence is reposed in an enterprise offering services to the public, which creates an opportunity for plunder, the enterprise is liable as an insurer. But the opinion does not read that way, and insofar as the general rule exceeds the bounds of the analogy between an inn and a steamboat, it is speculative and awaits another case in which other facts will or will not be found by analogy to be subject to the same rule. One might speculate, for example, about the liability of a stagecoach or a bus that carries passengers overnight; but, in view of the differences between an inn and a steamboat, on one hand, and a stagecoach or a bus, on the other, such speculation might go either way and would be far from certain. Brewer might respond that the AWR need not be so broad. It might not refer to anything more than innkeepers and steamboat operators: to wit, "When a person reposes great confidence in an innkeeper or a steamboat operator, in circumstances that create a great temptation to fraud and danger of plunder, the latter is liable as an insurer for the former's loss." That, however, leaves unexplained why such liability is confined to innkeepers and steamboat operators; it adopts the analogy's conclusion, while concealing the process of thought that produced it.

b. Statute: *Buck v. Jewell-LaSalle Realty Co.; Fortnightly Corp. v. United Artists Television, Inc.; Teleprompter Corp. v. Columbia Broadcasting System, Inc.; Twentieth Century Music Corp. v. Aiken*

Section 1 of the Copyright Act of 1909 provided: "Any person entitled thereto, upon complying with the provisions of this title, shall have the exclusive right...[t]o perform the copyrighted work publicly for profit if it be a musical composition."[13] In *Buck v. Jewell-LaSalle Realty Co.*,[14] the defendant, Jewell-LaSalle, operated a hotel in Kansas City. The hotel had a master radio receiving set, which was wired to its public and private rooms. It received broadcasts of a local radio station that included copyrighted songs of composers represented by the American Society of Composers, Authors, and Publishers (ASCAP) and transmitted the broadcasts to the hotel's rooms. The defendant was notified that it was infringing copyrights and, when the reception and transmission of the broadcasts continued, ASCAP sued for an injunction and damages. Relief was denied on the basis that the hotel's acts in receiving and transmitting programs broadcast by the radio station did not constitute a "performance" under the Act and were not, therefore, covered by the copyright. The plaintiffs appealed to the Circuit Court of Appeals, which certified

to the Supreme Court the question whether the hotel was performing the songs within the meaning of the Copyright Act. Among other arguments, the defendant contended that the reception and transmission of a program to its rooms was "no different from listening to a distant rendition of the same program."[15] Since the energy that activated the receiver was part of the same energy that was set in motion by the performer, the receiver was merely "a mechanical or electrical ear-trumpet for the better audition of a distant performance."[16]

The Supreme Court concluded otherwise. Sounds, it said, consist of waves that pass through the air and are locally audible. Music played at a broadcasting studio is not directly heard at a distant receiving set. The sound waves are transmitted as inaudible electrical currents – radio waves – that the receiver converts back into audible sound waves. The guests in the hotel did not, therefore, hear the original program as it was produced; they heard a reproduction of it. And the reproduction was a performance. "There is no difference in substance between the case where a hotel engages an orchestra to furnish the music and that where, by means of the radio set and loud-speakers here employed, it furnishes the same music for the same purpose. In each the music is produced by instrumentalities under its control."[17]

The Court's opinion is brief. Its conclusion rests entirely on the analogy it drew between a live hotel orchestra, performances of which were unquestionably covered by the copyright, and reception and transmission of a radio broadcast. The Court noted that there might be policy reasons why such activities should not be regarded as infringement of the copyright; but the Copyright Act did not so provide.[18] It observed further that Congress was then undertaking revisions of the Act.[19] Considerations of policy, in short, were not apposite. Having to decide whether the hotel's activities were more like *playing* the music or *listening* to it, the radio itself more like a microphone or a hearing aid, the Court drew on the analogy to a live orchestra, and the case was decided.

Thirty-seven years later, in *Fortnightly Corp. v. United Artists Television, Inc.*,[20] the Supreme Court revisited its holding in *Jewell-LaSalle*, in the context of television. Fortnightly operated community antenna television (CATV) systems, by which television programs of five stations were transmitted to homes in communities that the stations' own broadcasts did not reach. The programs included movies to which United Artists held the copyrights. The licenses that United Artists gave to the stations to show the movies did not authorize a further transmission. United Artists sued Fortnightly for copyright infringement. As in *Jewell-LaSalle*, the crucial question was whether Fortnightly had "performed" the movies.

Relying on the holding of the earlier case, the trial court and the court of appeals answered that it had. This time, however, the Supreme Court came out the other way. It said that although transmission of a television program was clearly not a performance in a conventional sense, the question could not be resolved by resort to ordinary meaning and legislative history; for television had been unknown when the Copyright Act was enacted.[21] Instead, the Court considered a number of examples of activities that were, or were not, regarded as performances under the Act and reasoned by analogy. Contrasting the exhibitor of a movie or play, who unquestionably performs, and a member of a theater audience, who unquestionably does not, and extending those examples to a television broadcaster, on one hand, and a television viewer, on the other, the Court concluded that Fortnightly, like a television viewer, was not an "active performer" but rather the "passive beneficiary" of the performance of another.[22] "Essentially," the Court said, "a CATV system no more than enhances the viewer's capacity to receive the broadcaster's signals. . . . CATV equipment is powerful and sophisticated, but the basic function the equipment serves is little different from that served by the equipment generally furnished by a television viewer."[23] A CATV system, that is to say, is more like a pair of binoculars than a movie projector. Reinforcing its conclusion, the Court noted a number of respects in which the function of a CATV system is unlike the function of a broadcaster.[24] Invited by the Solicitor General to reach a compromise decision that would accommodate considerations of copyright, communications, and antitrust policy, the Court declined the invitation; "[t]hat job," it said, "is for Congress."[25] As for the conflicting opinion in *Jewell-LaSalle*, it "must be understood as limited to its own facts."*[26]

The Court considered again whether a CATV system performs the television programs that it transmits six years later in *Teleprompter Corp. v. Columbia Broadcasting System, Inc.*[27] The plaintiffs argued that the case differed from *Fortnightly* in a number of respects, which, they said, made the defendants' activities of reception and transmission enough like broadcasting to count as a performance. Some of the CATV systems in this case originated their own programs, the function of an ordinary broadcaster; they sold advertising time, a characteristic of broadcasters; and they licensed some of their original programs to other CATV systems, again behaving like broadcasters.[28] Some of the defendants, like Fortnightly,

---

* Justice Fortas, dissenting, observed that applying the provisions of the Copyright Act to television, which did not exist when the Act was enacted, was "like trying to repair a television set with a mallet." *Fortnightly Corp. v. United Artists Television, Inc.*, 392 U.S. 403 (1968) (Fortas, J., dissenting). In the absence of congressional action, he favored adhering to the reasoning in *Jewell-LaSalle*, which, he said, might not be "an altogether ideal gloss on the word 'perform,'" but had "at least the merit of being settled law." Id. at 407.

transmitted programs beyond the range of the original broadcast, which also, the plaintiffs argued, made it akin to a broadcaster.[29]

None of that, the Court said, made any difference. Adhering to its reasoning in *Fortnightly*, the Court said that while analogies to the performance and viewing of live or filmed performances "were necessarily imperfect, a simple line could be drawn: 'Broadcasters perform. Viewers do not perform.'"[30] Although the CATV systems in this case had some of the trappings of a broadcaster, nevertheless they were more like viewers. As for the transmission of signals beyond the range of the original broadcast, that was still "essentially a viewer function, irrespective of the distance between the broadcasting station and the ultimate viewer."[31] The Court speculated a little about likely consequences of its holding for the television industry; but, it said, developing facts on which to base a sounder rule and framing such a rule were legislative, rather than judicial, functions and "beyond the competence of this Court."[32] "[R]esolution of the many sensitive and important problems in this field... must be left to Congress."[33] Dissenting in part, Justice Blackmun observed that the Court's "simple" analysis, "Broadcasters perform. Viewers do not perform," was "simplistic."[34] Justice Douglas, also dissenting, insisted that "[i]n any realistic practical sense" the activities of

CATV systems were broadcasting, not viewing, and should be so regarded.[35] *Fortnightly*, he said, should be limited "to its precise facts," as the Court had previously limited *Jewell-LaSalle*.[36]

The Supreme Court had one more opportunity to consider the question a year later, in *Twentieth Century Music Corp. v. Aiken*.[37] Aiken operated a fast food shop, in which he installed a radio with four speakers. Throughout the day, Aiken, his employees, and his customers heard whatever was broadcast on the station to which the radio was tuned. As in *Jewell-LaSalle*, the holders of copyrights to some of the songs that were broadcast sued for copyright infringement. Although this case involved radio, not television, and had nothing to do with cable transmission, the Court said that *Fortnightly* and *Teleprompter*, not *Jewell-LaSalle*, were controlling: "If, by analogy to a live performance in a concert hall or cabaret, a radio station 'performs' a musical composition when it broadcasts it, the same analogy would seem to require the conclusion that those who listen to the broadcast through the use of radio receivers do not perform the composition."[38] The Court noted some of the practical difficulties of applying a contrary rule and left it at that.

In all of these opinions, there was reference to the policy considerations that might point one way or the other and the possibility of a legislative solution, incidentally in *Jewell-LaSalle* and with increasing emphasis, either by the majority or the dissent, in the later opinions. However, the Court regarded itself as bound not to resolve the problem on policy grounds. Its task was to apply the statute before it, even though, as the Court observed in *Fortnightly*, the statute "was drafted long before the development of the electronic phenomena" that were at issue.[39] Performing its task, the Court relied first and foremost on analogies between an ordinary performer and a broadcaster, on one hand, and between a member of an ordinary, on-site audience and a radio listener or television viewer on the other. Insofar as instrumental arguments appear in the opinion, they are peripheral, not central, and are made not to supplant the analogies but to support them. Nor is there evident any general rule from which the controlling analogies can be derived. The shift from *Jewell-LaSalle* to the latter three cases, which required that it be "limited to its own facts," was little more than a reconfiguration of those analogies, without further explanation.* Were the analogies left aside, the opinions would have a gaping hole at their center.

---

* In the 1976 revision of the Copyright Act, Congress went the other way. The Act provides: "To 'perform' a work means to recite, render, play, dance, or act it, either directly or by means of any device or process...." 17 U.S.C. §101.

c. Constitution: *Olmstead v. United States;*
Katz v. United States

Olmstead was the leading figure in a conspiracy to bootleg liquor. The conspirators used the telephone to receive orders for the liquor and to arrange for delivery. Federal prohibition officers tapped the telephone lines of the main office of the conspiracy and the homes of four of the conspirators over a long period. The taps were made from outside the premises, without trespass on the conspirators' property. Evidence from the taps was used at the trial of Olmstead and other conspirators, over their objection that it had been obtained in violation of the Fourth Amendment and was therefore inadmissible. The defendants were convicted, and the convictions were affirmed on appeal.[40]

The Supreme Court affirmed. The larger part of the Court's opinion reviewed prior cases under the Fourth Amendment, all of which had involved the Government's search for and seizure of a document or tangible thing, rather than overhearing a private conversation, by telephone or otherwise. Having concluded its review, the Court said: "The Amendment itself shows that the search is to be of material things – the person, the house, his papers or his effects. The description of the warrant necessary to make the proceeding lawful, is that it must specify the place to be searched and the person or *things* to

[54]

be seized."[41] The defendants urged that the wiretapping was analogous to the Government's opening a sealed letter in the mail. Agreeing that opening a letter was a search and seizure, the Court rejected the analogy to wiretapping. A letter, it said, is "a paper, an effect."[42] In this case, however:

> There was no searching. There was no seizure. The evidence was secured by the use of the sense of hearing and that only. There was no entry of the houses or offices of the defendants.... The language of the Amendment can not be extended and expanded to include telephone wires reaching to the whole world from the defendant's house or office. The intervening wires are not part of his house or office any more than are the highways along which they are stretched.[43]

In the absence of "a seizure of [a defendant's] papers or his tangible material effects" or "an actual physical invasion of his house," the tapping of telephone lines is not "a search or seizure within the meaning of the Fourth Amendment."[44] Congress might protect the secrecy of telephone conversations by appropriate legislation, if it chose to do so.[45]

Dissenting, Justice Brandeis argued that the reference to "searches" and "seizures" in the Fourth Amendment should not be applied literally. In view of the purpose of the Amendment, which is to protect the individual's right to be let alone by the Government, "every unjustifiable intrusion by the

Government upon the privacy of the individual, whatever the means employed, must be deemed a violation."[46] From that point of view, it was irrelevant whether there was a physical entry or search; with respect to the crucial matter, the intrusion on privacy, the two situations were alike – analogous – and the same rule should be applied to both. Brandeis pointed to other cases, none of them involving a telephone tap or oral communication of any kind, in which the notion of a search and seizure had been interpreted expansively to carry out the Amendment's purpose.* Justices Butler and Stone agreed.† Justice Butler observed: "Tapping the wires and listening in by the officers literally constituted a search for evidence. As the communications passed, they were heard and taken down."[47]

Almost forty years later, the Supreme Court revisited the issue of wiretapping in *Katz v. United States*.[48] Katz, a bookmaker, was convicted of transmitting wagering information by telephone. At trial, the government introduced evidence of his end of conversations that he had made from a telephone booth. Government agents had overheard and recorded what he said by a device attached to the outside of the booth.

---

* *Olmstead v. United States*, 277 U.S. 438, 475–477 (1928) (Brandeis, J., dissenting). The cases that Brandeis mentioned involved opening a sealed letter that had been deposited in the mail, the production of a document in response to a subpoena, and the taking of papers from an office by a friendly visitor.
† Id. at 485, 488. The fourth dissenter was Justice Holmes, whose opinion went off on another ground.

The Government contended that the Fourth Amendment was inapplicable, there having been no physical penetration of the telephone booth and no seizure of tangible property.* The Court disagreed. Citing a case decided after *Olmstead*,[49] it said that the Amendment extended to the recording of oral statements and might apply even if there was no trespass. Adopting Brandeis's view in *Olmstead*, the Court said that the key was not property but privacy. "The Government's activities in electronically listening to and recording the petitioner's words violated the privacy upon which he justifiably relied while using the telephone booth and thus constituted a 'search and seizure' within the meaning of the Fourth Amendment."[50]

Justice Black dissented. The Fourth Amendment's language, he said, "connote[s] the idea of tangible things with size, form, and weight, things capable of being searched, seized, or both. . . . A conversation overheard by eavesdropping, whether by plain snooping or wiretapping is not tangible

---

* That position was, of course, supported by *Olmstead*. The Government relied principally on a case decided after *Olmstead*, *Goldman v. United States*, 316 U.S. 129 (1942), in which the Court had upheld the admissibility of evidence obtained by placing a listening device against the other side of a wall of the defendant's office. See p. 85. Taking note of criticism of the *Goldman* decision, the Government argued also that, even if a trespass were not required, a public telephone booth was not a "constitutionally protected area," i.e., the Fourth Amendment did not apply at all to intrusions into the booth. Brief for the Respondent at 14–17, *Katz v. United States*, 389 U.S. 347 (1967) (No. 35). Declaring in a much-quoted aphorism that "the Fourth Amendment protects people, not places," *Katz v. United States*, 389 U.S. 347, 351 (1967), the Court rejected that argument.

and, under the normally accepted meanings of the words, can neither be searched nor seized."[51] Furthermore, eavesdropping was not unknown when the Fourth Amendment was drafted. Had the Framers intended that it be included within the Fourth Amendment, Black believed, "they would have used the appropriate language to do so."[52] To apply language directed at searches and seizures to eavesdropping was, he said, "clever word juggling."[53]

The word "analogy" is not used in *Katz*; but it might well have been. The words of the Fourth Amendment do not apply literally to eavesdropping, because, just as Black said, one would not ordinarily refer to searching or seizing what is only spoken. The nub of the Court's argument was that, in light of the purpose of the Fourth Amendment, eavesdropping is analogous to a search and seizure, and the analogy is close enough to call for the same result. Making the analogy more concrete by reference to prior cases, it said: "No less than an individual in a business office, in a friend's apartment, or in a taxicab, a person in a telephone booth may rely upon the protection of the Fourth Amendment."[54] Neither the Court nor Justice Black had much to say for or against the exclusion of evidence obtained by wiretapped conversations as a matter of policy, although some of the concurring opinions referred briefly to cases involving national security.[55] Insofar as instrumental considerations of that kind were taken into account, it was only to show that the analogy itself was sound.

One can find in the opinion in *Katz* the statement of a general principle from which the result is drawn. It is because the eavesdropping "violated the privacy upon which [Katz] justifiably relied while using the telephone booth" that it was a search and seizure.[56] That proposition has generally been regarded as the crux of the case. It is not unqualified, however. Elsewhere, the Court said:

> [T]he Fourth Amendment cannot be translated into a general constitutional "right to privacy." That Amendment protects individual privacy against certain kinds of governmental intrusion, but its protections go further, and often have nothing to do with privacy at all. Other provisions of the Constitution protect personal privacy from other forms of governmental invasion. But the protection of a person's *general* right to privacy – his right to be let alone by other people – is, like the protection of his property and of his very life, left largely to the law of the individual States.[57]

The reason why *this* invasion of Katz's privacy constituted a search and seizure although other invasions might not is provided by the analogy that the Court drew between the telephone booth from which Katz spoke and "a business office...a friend's apartment...or...a taxicab." It is easy to overlook the analogy, because the privacy at stake seems so obvious, in comparison with other aspects of privacy that the Court mentioned.* But, as Justice Black's dissenting opinion makes plain, without the analogy, the Court's argument is incomplete.

In none of the foregoing cases does the analogy on which the Court primarily relied disappear from view, as it does in Brewer's account. Nor could it. For it is a crucial part of the argument. Were the comparison with an innkeeper eliminated in *Adams*, the comparisons with live performance and listening or viewing eliminated in *Jewell-LaSalle* and the other cases, the comparison with a physical search eliminated in *Olmstead* and *Katz*, the opinions would collapse. In each of the cases, it is possible to reject the analogy without logical error, as the dissenting Justices in the latter two sets of cases showed. But it cannot simply be shelved or displaced; nor can it be reconstructed as an inductive and/or deductive argument, without transforming it altogether. The opinions give no sign that the judges are uncomfortable with their reasoning, or that, as Sunstein suggests,† they argued as they did because they were

---

* E.g., privacy of association and the prohibition of unconsented peacetime quartering of soldiers, protected respectively by the First and Third Amendment. *Katz*, 389 U.S. at 350 n.5. The analogy between eavesdropping and a search and seizure of tangible objects is all the more obvious now because it has been applied repeatedly in the thirty-eight years since *Katz*.
† See p. 30.

unable to agree on what would be a sound policy or instrumental arguments to achieve it. On the contrary, they studiously avoid embarking on that kind of inquiry, because it was not necessary to the argument being made and also, most explicitly in the broadcasting cases, because it was inappropriate to their task.

If one attends to scholarly writings about the use of analogical arguments in legal reasoning, the opinions in all these cases are radically defective. Absent from all of them is a clear statement of a general, fully dispositive principle that the court is applying, indeed, in the view of some critics of analogical argument, must be applying, if the court is to be credited with having reasoned at all. The opinions themselves offer little support for that view. Any principle that a court offers appears not to reach further than what is required by a comparison of the specific facts before the court with other facts, equally specific, for which the result is known. So, although in *Adams*, the court evidently thought that the passengers' reliance on the steamboat operator and the operator's temptation to betray that confidence were significant, it went no further than to conclude that, in view of those facts, the relationship between operator and passengers was like the relationship between an innkeeper and his guests. It did not purport to say what the outcome would be if another form of transportation were involved or in any other kind of situation in which one person reposes confidence in another who is tempted to betray it. In the broadcasting cases, the Court did not attempt to catalogue every kind of technological feat that would or would not constitute a "performance" under the provisions of the copyright law. It was able to distinguish the decision in *Jewell-LaSalle* from the three cases that followed it precisely because in the earlier case it had not laid down a rule for broadcasting generally. In the latter series of cases as well, there was need for two further opinions after *Fortnightly* was decided because the Court had not in that case declared a general rule for every manner of broadcast transmission of radio and television or even for CATV systems alone.

Olmstead and *Katz* appear to come closest to the statement of a general rule. But the opinions in those cases as well are more narrowly focused. "The [Fourth] Amendment," the Court said in *Olmstead*, "does not forbid *what was done here*."[58] Overruling *Olmstead*, the Court said in *Katz* that "what [a person] seeks to preserve as private, even in an area accessible to the public, *may* be constitutionally protected."[59] Tailoring its conclusion to the facts of the case, it said: "[A] person in a telephone booth may rely upon the protection of the Fourth Amendment. One who occupies it, shuts the door behind him, and pays the toll that permits him to place a call is surely entitled to assume that the words he utters into the mouthpiece will not be broadcast to the world."[60] What the result would be if the person left the door to the booth open, or if he called from one of a row of unenclosed public telephones, or in any of the other circumstances to which the initial general proposition might apply, the Court did not say. If, in the course of comparing eavesdropping on Katz's conversation in the telephone booth to other situations to which the Fourth Amendment applied, the Court referred to a "legitimate expectation of privacy," that phrase was more a generalization from specific results than a principle leading to them; and even as such, it left abundant opportunity for further distinctions, as later cases showed.* The familiar practice of *distinguishing* a prior case from the one presently before a court, as in *Fortnightly*, depends on such reticence. To be sure, one might speculate what the result would be were an analogous case to arise; but such speculation, like the court's reasoning, would depend on the relevance of the analogy.

---

* The phrase "legitimate expectation of privacy," which became the rubric for identification of a Fourth Amendment interest, see *Rakas v. Illinois*, 439 U.S. 128, 143 (1978), is derived (inexactly) from Justice Harlan's concurring opinion in *Katz*, 389 U.S. at 360. The opinion for the Court in *Katz* made the same point, somewhat more obliquely. Id. at 352. When there is, or is not, a legitimate expectation of privacy became a major topic of Fourth Amendment jurisprudence. See *Rakas*, above; *Minnesota v. Carter*, 525 U.S. 83 (1998).

CHAPTER THREE

Analogical Legal Reasoning

The use of analogies in the cases discussed in Chapter 2 is strongly at odds with accounts of analogical reasoning that treat it, one way or another, as suspect: either a flawed and inadequate (even if somehow useful) substitute for the real thing or a preliminary and ultimately disposable stimulus to a sound argument, which contributes nothing to the argument's validity. In all of the cases, the court relied on analogical reasoning much more forcefully than that, as an integral part of the argument itself. Much of the discussion in the opinions is deployed to vindicate the court's reliance on one analogy rather than another. Dissenting judges express their objection to the majority's conclusion as disagreement with the analogy on which the majority relies, and they offer an alternative analogy that seems to them more persuasive. Far from analogies serving merely to illustrate or underscore an instrumental argument, such arguments from prior cases are used to explain why the analogy is a good one, and the analogy in turn supports reliance on those instrumental arguments. If the court expresses a general principle that expands on an analogy ("Broadcasters perform; viewers do not perform," "Privacy protects people, not places"), on its own the principle is too broad to express the court's holding and requires reference to the analogy to ascertain its true scope. The direction of thought is from the analogy to the principle, rather than the other way around.

The dismissive treatment of analogical arguments is not, then, based simply on a close reading of judicial opinions, which themselves betray no doubt or diffidence about their use. Nor is it based on any special formal feature of legal reasoning in particular that makes the use of analogical arguments inappropriate; on the contrary, their use in legal reasoning is especially pronounced. Rather, it follows from a tacit or express assumption that only arguments with the credentials of deductive or inductive reasoning are weighty enough to count. Because an argument that depends on an analogy satisfies neither of those forms, it is concluded that the analogy must serve some other cognitive or rhetorical function or is only a placeholder for a different argument in proper form. From that perspective, the pervasive use of analogies in legal reasoning is a curiosity of the law, interesting perhaps, useful or not, and inviting explanation, but having little to do with fundamental legal concerns. For some, like Brewer, an analogy is something like a cognitive spark plug, which is no longer needed once the engine of reason turns over. Others, like Levi and Sunstein, promote the virtues of analogical reasoning, which, however, are not those of reasoned argument but rather the political benefits of selling reason short. Posner suggests that the prevalence of analogical reasoning is due to slipshod judicial work habits and a failure to come to grips with the real issues. The phantasm school, Alexander and others, dismisses even the possibility of an analogical argument, regarding it as a figment of our confused logical imaginations. What purports to be analogical reasoning, they say, is either an ordinary deductive inference or is not properly regarded as reasoning at all.

Because the criticism of analogical reasoning in the law takes this form, its defense has to proceed in stages. I begin in this chapter with examples of the use of analogical reasoning in our everyday lives, simply to show in the most direct way that it can be done: we do it all the time. Building on those examples as well as the cases presented in Chapter 2, I discuss the use of analogical arguments in the law and the manner in which analogical legal argument intersects with the model of legal reasoning as a coherent, deductively ordered hierarchy of rules. I then consider the objections to this account of legal reasoning in more detail. In Chapter 4, drawing on work in epistemology and cognitive psychology, I sketch how we reason analogically, not to instruct those who do not already know, for instruction is not needed – the critics of analogical arguments assuredly rely on them, along with the rest of us – but to meet the challenge that, despite all appearances to the contrary, it cannot be done.

a. Practical analogical reasoning

Mary spills cranberry juice on a white tablecloth. "Try pouring salt on it," Edna says. "It works with wine."

Charlie cannot start his lawn mower. It occurs to him that when his car does not start, it sometimes helps to turn off the motor and let it stand for a while. He goes inside to watch television.

Although they are not likely to notice it or to make much of it if they do, Edna and Charlie are reasoning by analogy. Observing the similarity between (red) wine and cranberry juice – both are red and liquid – and knowing that salt helps to remove a wine stain, Edna speculates that cranberry juice shares that characteristic with wine as well. Knowing that his lawn mower and his car are both powered by internal combustion engines (or perhaps only that both engines use gasoline for fuel) and that sometimes when his car does not start, it is because he has flooded the engine, Charlie speculates that that is why his lawn mower does not start, and he waits for the excess gasoline to evaporate.

In countless situations of everyday life, we engage in practical analogical reasoning of this kind. Most of the time, confronting a problem that is not just like one that we have encountered before, we neither embark on a program of experiments to discover what will work nor do research in the appropriate field to learn the applicable general rule. There is not time for that, and even if there were, ordinarily it would not be time well spent. Rather, we make an educated guess, based on our experience of situations that are more or less similar. Very likely, we could not offer any rule or principle that justifies the guess; it is the past experience itself on which we rely. Unless Edna happens to be a food chemist, she probably does not know why salt removes a wine stain. She knows only that it does and relies on the fact that cranberry juice also is a red liquid. If Mary asked her to explain why salt has that effect, Edna might respond, "I don't know, it just does," or she might say something conclusory like, "I suppose it absorbs the wine," and let it go at that. If the stain were blood, she might not recommend salt – blood is a red liquid, but it seems less like wine in other respects – and if it were chocolate ice cream, she probably would not, although a stain is a stain and, absent any better idea, why not? Charlie need not know why flooding the engine prevents a car or, as he speculates, a lawn mower, from starting or even know, except in the most general terms, what "flooding the engine" means; nor need he know why letting the engine sit "unfloods" it. If he were an auto mechanic or a small engine repairman, he would know more. But for his purposes, it is enough to know that the engines of a car and a lawn mower are more or less similar.

The similarities that prompt Edna and Charlie to reason analogically are, of course, accompanied by many dissimilarities. Without giving it a thought, Edna no doubt assumed that the absorbent capacity of salt would not be affected by the fact that wine is more expensive than cranberry juice, or that the wine that was spilled the other time was imported and cranberry juice is not. Were she asked why she made those assumptions, she would most likely be puzzled, because it all seems so obvious. Charlie may know very little about cars or small engines. Nevertheless, almost certainly it will not occur to him that the lawn mower may not work the way his car does because it is red and the car is blue. How does he know that? Well, everyone knows that the color of a machine has nothing to do with how its engine works. If, when Charlie told his wife that the lawn mower would not start and he was going inside to watch television, she were to reply, "What's the good of that? Try kicking it. That gets a donkey started," Charlie would most likely go on inside, even though a lawn mower and a donkey are more similar in some respects than a lawn mower and a car. They just do not seem very much alike for *this* purpose. Kicking a lawn mower *might* help to start it; but it does not seem likely.

In a sense, practical analogical reasoning is "incompletely theorized," as Sunstein describes the outcome of analogical legal reasoning.* Most of the time, however, it would be more accurate to say that it is not theorized at all. Edna and Charlie have practical problems, for which their experience suggests practical solutions. Having gotten that far, a theory is beside the point. The observed similarity between past experience and present problem or, in the language of analogy, between source and target is itself enough to prompt the connection between them, without mediation by a general rule.† If they were asked to frame a rule from which the solution followed as a deductive inference, very likely they would not know how to proceed, unless they simply constructed a rule out of the

---

* See p. 30.
† From the perspective of cognitive psychology, the matter is a good deal more complex. There have been many experiments and much has been written about what makes an effective analogy, either drawn from one's own experience and knowledge or presented as the solution to one problem and recognized as a possible solution to another, different problem. Such explanations are the cognitive face of explanations in terms of causal connectedness or, simply, relevance, to which I have referred elsewhere. See pp. 124–133.

source and target themselves: "Salt removes stains caused by wine and cranberry juice," "If a car or a lawn mower won't start, letting it stand a while may help." A more general rule might occur to them – "Salt removes red stains," "Letting an engine stand for a while may help to start it" – or a more informative rule – "Salt absorbs liquids, which carry some of the staining pigment with them," "Letting excess gasoline evaporate helps to start an engine." But it would make no difference. For they are interested for the moment in solving a particular problem, and speculation beyond that is not to the purpose. Were they obliged to conduct an empirical inquiry in order to frame a rule from which they could deduce a solution to the problem at hand, they would be stymied altogether. Of course, their ready solutions may turn out to be mistaken.* If the matter were of sufficient importance and there were time, they might try to confirm their solutions inductively before applying them. If, for example, Mary's tablecloth were a family heirloom, she might want to try Edna's suggestion on a white rag before pouring salt on the tablecloth. In a matter

---

* As it happens, salt is as effective – not very – on a cranberry juice stain as on a red wine stain. It works as an absorbent. When it absorbs the liquid from the stained cloth, it also absorbs some of a water-soluble compound called an anthocyanin, which accounts for the red color of both red wine and cranberry juice. Other methods of removing stains would also be equally effective on both. But Edna will be disappointed if she presses her analogical reasoning too far. The pigmentation of tomatoes and watermelons is different, and stains from them require different treatment.

of very great importance, one might insist on understanding how a solution works and formulating a rule (which might be a good deal broader than the particular problem requires) from which the solution follows deductively. But for ordinary affairs, the analogy itself is enough.

Practical analogical reasoning allows a person to take considered action and to achieve his purposes over a vastly larger range than would otherwise be possible. Without the capacity to reason in this way and to base one's actions on the outcome, a person would be effectively immobilized, except when the similarity between a present problem and past experience is so great that they are for practical purposes the same.* Without resort to analogical reasoning, how would Edna go about removing the stain from her tablecloth, unless she had a book that told how to remove stains, cranberry juice in particular? How would Charlie, using a lawn mower for the first time and flooding the engine, get the job done, unless there were a neighbor who had used a lawn mower and could advise him? How would the neighbor have learned what to do, and how would he know that what works for his lawn mower will work for Charlie's, which is not the same model? Far from being

---

* They would, of course, not be literally the same. There is no clear line between sameness and similarity, for no two things are alike or unlike in all respects. To say that two phenomena are "the same" is itself to display the capacity to distinguish relevant and irrelevant similarities and differences that figures so large in analogical reasoning. See pp. 124–126.

special to the law, analogical reasoning is used by all of us constantly, to conduct the most ordinary affairs. Our lives depend on it.

Whatever success Edna, Charlie, and the rest of us have in using analogical reasoning to solve the small crises of everyday life, those who dismiss or decry its use in the law are not likely to be convinced that such success has anything to do with their concerns. The off-the-cuff, practical problem solving in which we all engage will appear to them an odd model for the rulings of a court. In the first place, the nature of the tasks is different. Edna and Charlie require specific information about what is the case, more particularly, how things work. A court, on the other hand, determines the rights and duties of the parties; it prescribes behavior. (The tasks are not always so unalike. We commonly use analogical reasoning to resolve a question about how one ought to behave or ought to have behaved in a specific situation. Such a question is prescriptive, like the question before a court.)

Likewise, the manner of going about the tasks is different. The lessons of ordinary experience like those on which Edna and Charlie rely are mostly acquired and applied in haphazard, episodic fashion, even if they are sometimes gathered into workaday practices that have some of the quality of rules. The law, on the other hand, is organized systematically into a body of rules set forth as "black letter law," codes, re-statements,* and the like, which are available for examination and intended for use in future cases. A judicial decision of any significance is carefully considered and is not likely to be reached until the issue has been debated and alternative outcomes forcefully defended. Once rendered, it is subject to review and reconsideration by other judges as well as by lawyers and legal scholars.† Furthermore, adjudication is constrained by formal procedures that have no counterpart in daily life. A procedural irregularity may itself be the ground for invalidating an outcome, however persuasive it is on its own terms. (In contrast, even if one thought that Mary would be foolish not to try salt first on something less valuable than her best tablecloth, so long as the stain is removed, Edna will not be faulted.) So also, having to deal with a stained tablecloth or a balky lawn mower and the like, we are not likely to think at all about how the action that we take then will affect what

---

* "Restatements" are codifications of case law in a general area. They are the product of The American Law Institute, a private foundation based in Philadelphia, which includes among its members leading lawyers, judges, and law professors. Restatements are drafted by a committee and are finally approved by the membership as a whole. Although they have no formal legal authority, they are given great weight and are often cited in judicial opinions.

† Judges on the same court or a lower court in the same jurisdiction may be bound to adhere to a prior ruling. But there is usually some scope for them to consider what a prior ruling actually was and to "distinguish" the cases. In any event, judges who are not so bound commonly refer to rulings in other cases and consider them on the merits.

we do thereafter. No doubt, if the solution works, we shall use it again, if the same problem recurs, or we may (reasoning analogically) apply it to a different but similar problem (red jelly). But for the moment, our concern is confined to the matter at hand; the problem and the solution are particular, not general. Although a judicial decision also is particular – it decides that case and no other – its implications are general; it bespeaks a rule, grounded in the past and extending into the future.

All of these differences point to a further, overriding difference. If, on the one hand, the solution to an everyday practical problem is likely to be reached without extensive study or formal procedure and without consideration beyond the concrete problem itself, on the other hand, it can generally be put to the test directly and definitively. Mary's tablecloth comes clean; Charlie's lawn mower starts, or it does not. And since nothing else is at stake, there is no more to be said. In adjudication, the situation is reversed. The deliberation and procedural formality that precede the decision and the concern to reach a result that will be satisfactory for similar problems in the future are not paralleled after the decision by any definite criteria of its correctness.* The lack of such a test, no doubt, accounts in

---

* An appellate court may, of course, declare that the lower court's decision was correct or incorrect. But there is then no test of the correctness of the appellate court's decision, unless it is subject to review by a still higher court.

large measure for the attention to the process by which the decision is reached, as well as the scholarly insistence that analogical reasoning be replaced with more rigorous logical forms. Notwithstanding the many aspects of legal argument and decision that have no counterpart in daily life, however, the form of reasoning – deriving the solution to a problem from the solution to another problem, on the basis of a similarity between them – is the same in both. Furthermore, while the use of analogical reasoning in ordinary affairs is a likely and highly serviceable expedient, in adjudication it is more than that. It is indispensable.

b. Legal reasoning

It should first be made explicit what has up to now been taken for granted. "Legal reasoning," as that term is usually used and as I have used it here, refers to the reasoning pattern of lawyers when they argue a case and judges when they decide one. It does not refer to the reasoning of legislators and their aides arguing in support of or in opposition to legislation or of administrative officials when they take steps to enforce the law, although they all reason about the law and almost certainly make use of analogies. The adjudicative task of a court is to determine the outcome of a specific, concrete controversy in all its particularity. In this respect, it is quite different from legislation, the objective of which, even if it is prompted by particular circumstances, is to fashion a rule of general application for all instances of a designated type. So also, it is different from executive action, which is invoked to implement a determinate outcome in a particular instance.* The difference in function explains why, although analogical reasoning is useful in legal matters generally as it is elsewhere, it has a special role in adjudication.

The starting point for an adjudicative decision is the actual facts of a controversy between two (or sometimes more) parties. This aspect of legal reasoning, implicit in the very meaning of adjudication, is manifest in the common provision that limits a court's jurisdiction to a "case or controversy."† As a matter of course, lawyers' briefs and oral arguments begin with a statement of the facts of the case. So also do judicial opinions.‡ Those facts, that case, are what bring the

---

* In practice, the differences among adjudication, legislation, and administration are not so clear. Administrative agencies in particular often perform functions partaking of all three. Nevertheless, they are expected to perform their various functions in a manner that reflects the kind of function being performed.

† See U.S. Const., Art. III, §2. The requirement of a case or controversy may be weakened by provisions for a court to answer a hypothetical question or a request for an "advisory opinion" from some other governmental body. The Constitution of Massachusetts, amend. 85, for example, provides: "Each branch of the legislature, as well as the governor or the council, shall have authority to require the opinions of the justices of the supreme judicial court, upon important questions of law, and upon solemn occasions."

‡ Chief Justice Warren's opinion in *Miranda v. Arizona*, 384 U.S. 436 (1966), is a rare exception, one of the reasons why the Supreme Court's pronouncement of

lawyers and judge into court; that, for the moment, is their only business together. Only a small number of the details of the situation out of which the controversy arises will affect the outcome; but all the details are potentially available for consideration, because it is that specific situation and no other that needs to be resolved. The lawyers' arguments and the judge's opinion recite only those facts that they respectively believe are material to the outcome. Although there are likely to be facts the relevance of which is disputed, there are a great many others the relevance or, more likely, the lack of relevance of which is not in doubt. In *Adams*, neither of the lawyers (so far as we know) nor the Court of Appeals thought it necessary to mention the purpose of the plaintiff's trip, or what he had eaten for dinner, or whether it rained on the night in question, although any of those facts *might* have been relevant in other circumstances.* Those facts and myriad other details about that particular situation – Adams's trip upriver – were disregarded; but they were available to be considered, if the lawyer for one side or the other or the court had thought them relevant.

the "Miranda rules," having to do with police interrogation of a criminal suspect, was heavily criticized as being "legislative" rather than "judicial."

* If Adams's purpose in making the trip had been to deliver stolen property, would that have made a difference? Or if he had drunk a great deal of wine at dinner? Or if there had been a thunderstorm while he slept? Possibly none of those facts would in itself have affected the outcome. But with sufficient ingenuity, one can imagine them, together with other facts, making a difference.

A second distinctive feature of adjudication is that the court's decision is to be based entirely on the law. A great deal has been written about this requirement, both what it means and how it is carried out. In principle it is straightforward and, indeed, obvious. For the question that brings the parties into court is what *the law* obligates each of them to do with respect to one another in the circumstances, not, except insofar as their legal obligations may implicate such questions, how they can best accomplish their individual or mutual goals or, the law aside, what goals they ought to pursue or what will advance the interests of society generally. (Mary would not seek a judicial decision about how to remove that stain, but if Edna had stained the tablecloth and done nothing about it, Mary might ask a court to declare Edna's legal obligation to replace it. Charlie would not ask a judge how to start his lawn mower, but if he were convinced that it was defective, he might ask a court to declare that the store that sold it to him was legally obligated to repair or replace it.) What are appropriate sources of the law is a question about which there is much disagreement, but no one doubts that a court is to look to those sources and nowhere else.* Nor is it permissible to

---

* John Chipman Gray, *The Nature and Sources of the Law* (2d ed. 1921), now regarded as a classic of jurisprudence, is a good introduction to the subject of the proper sources of a legal decision. Benjamin N. Cardozo, *The Nature of the Judicial Process* (1921), another classic, is an excellent general discussion. More recent discussions of the same subject are contained in works

conclude that there is no law that disposes of the controversy before the court, which must therefore remain unresolved. A judge who can find no statute or judicial precedent that deals directly with the matter before her does not throw up her hands and tell the litigants to fight it out.*

It is a commonplace among trial lawyers that most legal controversies arise because the parties have different views about the facts and that once all the factual questions are resolved the case is easily decided. Sometimes, indeed, once the facts are known, the applicable rule of law is so clear that

about legal interpretation generally, as to which see p. 14 and references cited.

Adherents of Legal Realism and Critical Legal Studies, see p. 8n., questioned whether the sources of law in adjudication are different from the sources of legislation and social policy generally. See, e.g., Karl N. Llewellyn, *Some Realism About Realism – Responding to Dean Pound*, 44 Harv. L. Rev. 1222 (1931); Roberto Mangabeira Unger, *The Critical Legal Studies Movement* (1986). To rather different effect, some theories of law and the relation between law and morality urge that moral and political principles that have not been enacted into positive law are among the sources to which a judge should refer. See, e.g., Ronald Dworkin, *Taking Rights Seriously* 81–130 (1977). Such theories do not contradict the proposition that the sources of the answer to a question about the correct legal outcome of a controversy must be found within the law. Rather, they assert that the principles in question are implicit in the law or, at any rate, are unavoidably bound up in its correct interpretation. The question whether there is an articulable set of definite moral and political principles that are part of the law itself is near the heart of the debate between most schools of natural law and legal positivism. See pp. 152–158. For a different account of the division between the two, see Lloyd L. Weinreb, *Natural Law and Justice* 97–126, 259–263 (1987).

* In the absence of a settled rule that prescribes an outcome, it may appear that the judge must fill the gap by exercising her discretion, informed by considerations outside the law. It is true that a judge has more discretion in such a case. Nonetheless, her obligation is to decide according to the law. The method of analogical reasoning enables her to do so. See p. 98.

the court has nothing to do but state the rule and announce its decision.* A great many cases are resolved in that way. Much the greater number of legal obligations, after all, are uncontroversial and are never brought into court, because the parties recognize their mutual obligations and perform them. Tenants pay the rent, employers pay their employees' wages, borrowers return what they have borrowed, without resort to adjudication. Shared life in a community would be impossible otherwise.

If the facts as determined do not fall clearly under a dispositive rule, each side will seek to present the facts and the law in a light consistent with the outcome it favors. Facts and law are closely intertwined; for unless the applicable rules provide that certain facts make a difference to the outcome, there is no reason to dispute them. That is why no issue was made of what Adams ate for dinner on the night his money was stolen, even though, perhaps, he and the steward had different recollections of what was served. So, having an eye to the law, a lawyer will not only emphasize facts that support his client's position and minimize those that do not, but also, so far as the facts permit, will *characterize* them in a manner that calls for application of a rule that favors his client's position. At the same time, having an eye to the facts, he will emphasize

---

* Even in such a case, reasoning by analogy is not altogether absent, although it may be unnoticed. See p. 93n.

on a triviality – "the depth of the penetration of the electronic device" – rather than the invasion of privacy, which was the same whatever kind of electronic equipment was employed.[6] In *Katz*, mindful of the result in the earlier case, the federal agents who put the eavesdropping device in place had not penetrated the wall of the telephone booth;[7] so if anything remained of the requirement of a trespass, the eavesdropping could not easily have been described as a search and seizure. Instead, following Justice Douglas's line of reasoning, the Court modified the rule and enlarged the meaning of "search and seizure" to include eavesdropping without any physical intrusion in the circumstances of that case.*[8]

Having the facts of a case before him and looking within the body of the law for a ground of decision, the task of the lawyer or judge is first to locate the facts within a broad area

rules of law that favor his client's position and, so far as the rules permit, will *interpret* them in a manner that supports that position. Adjusting the characterization of the facts and the interpretation of the law mutually to one another, the lawyer's objective is to weave the two together into a coherent account pointing to the conclusion that the law applied to those facts dictates but one outcome. The opposing lawyer will make the same effort in the same manner, but she will, of course, direct her argument toward a different outcome.

In *Adams*, there was no rule that expressly defined the liability of steamboat operators, and the general rule was that a person is not liable for another person's loss unless it is due to the former's negligence. Innkeepers were subject to a stricter rule, which made them liable as an insurer, that is, without proof of negligence, for their guests' losses. It was, therefore, in the interest of the plaintiff to emphasize that the steamboat on which Adams took passage provided overnight lodging, like an inn, and to disregard the fact that it was not a building at all but a means of transportation that went up and down river, as an inn certainly does not. Bringing the facts to the rule, as it were, was evidently easier than bringing the rule to the facts and arguing directly that the rule about an innkeeper's liability was intended and should be understood to refer not only to innkeepers but also to the operator of a steamboat carrying passengers upriver overnight. Whichever the argument, the

---

* Bringing the facts within the rule has its limits. There is a well-known anecdote about a dean of Worcester College at Oxford University, who lived on the grounds of the college and kept a dog named Flint in his rooms. Someone was said to have objected, because a university regulation excluded dogs from college grounds. According to the story, the dean responded, "Sir, my dog is a cat." See John Walsh, "Harry's Dogs," in Lesley Le Claire, *For Harry* 54, 57–58 (Abbey Press, Abingdon 2001). The dog remained in the dean's rooms; but one may believe that the dean's reply stretched the limits of language and its interpretation to – or beyond – the breaking point. The strict classification of animal species makes it difficult, without tongue in cheek, to urge that a dog is a cat; but if Flint had been a good mouser, who knows? The dean's response would have been less remarkable if, instead of characterizing the facts to make his point, he had interpreted the law and said, in the manner of a legal argument, that despite the unqualified language of the regulation, it was not intended to apply to college officers or to the dean, or that the prohibition against dogs did not include very small dogs or dogs that are well-behaved.

outcome that it supported, which the plaintiff favored, was the same. The defendant's lawyers, on the other hand, would have emphasized the difference between an inn, stationary on land, and a steamboat traveling upriver and the similarity between the latter and a railroad sleeping car, an operator of which was not subject to the stricter liability rule.

In its opinion, the court adopted the plaintiff's characterization of the steamboat and called it "for all practical purposes, a floating inn," "one of the modern floating palaces that...navigate the interior waters of the country."[1] With that analogy in place, the rule about an innkeeper's liability became applicable and the rule about the liability of the operator of a railroad sleeping car, which might have been thought relevant, became inapt. At the same time, the court made a nod in the direction of the plaintiff's alternative argument. If the innkeepers' rule did not apply in terms to steamboat operators, still "the same considerations of public policy apply."[2]

Similarly, in *Katz*, considering the electronic eavesdropping of Katz's telephone conversation and confronted by the rule of *Olmstead* that a search and seizure under the Fourth Amendment involves a trespass, the Court might have taken either of two routes toward its holding that the eavesdropping was a violation of his constitutional right. It might have relied on a factual analogy and declared that the eavesdropping was

a trespass (or was "constructively" a trespass or was trespass"*), thus bringing the facts of the case withir of *Olmstead*, or it might have declared, as it did, that and seizure under the Fourth Amendment does not ily include a physical trespass, thereby expanding tł embrace the facts. Just six years earlier, in another so unlike *Katz*, the Court had adopted the former ra Police officers gained access to a vacant row hous ing premises that they believed were used as headqu an illegal gambling operation. By means of a "spike serted into the common wall between the houses, wł in contact with a heating duct of the suspect house, t able to overhear conversations that took place ther guishing another case in which the Court had held tha ing a listening device to a common wall without pene did *not* constitute a search and seizure,[4] the Court em that the spike mike had been stuck *into* the wall and, r analogically, concluded that this "unauthorized phys etration into the premises" occupied by the defenda fied the trespass requirement of a search and seizure or not there was a technical trespass under the local law."[5] In a concurring opinion, Justice Douglas object Court's rationale, which, he argued, made such case:

* "Constructively" and "quasi-" mean roughly "might as well have beer

of the law dealing with that kind of human conduct, and then, including more and more particular detail, progressively to sharpen the focus until there emerges a rule that applies squarely to those facts. Ordinarily, the relevant area of the law is quickly and easily determined, because the categories of the law correspond, as they must, to the kinds of controversies that arise. Occasionally, the facts of a case do not lie neatly within one clearly defined category or another but fall on the border between two well-defined categories, so that rules of law from both may alike have some bearing on the outcome.* The familiar legal categories – torts, contract, criminal law, environmental law, securities regulation, and so forth – are, in any event, not rigid and mutually exclusive but are rather conventional rubrics that refer to a grouping of rules related together by the kind of conduct with which they deal.† As

---

* See, for example, *Crisci v. Security Insurance Co. of New Haven, Conn.*, 426 P.2d 173 (Cal. 1967), in which the plaintiff, who suffered a large judgment against her in a personal injury action, sued the defendant, her insurer, for refusing to settle the claim at a much lower figure, within the amount of the insurance policy. The plaintiff claimed damages including an amount for mental suffering. Upholding an award of damages to the plaintiff that included compensation for the amount of the judgment against her and for her mental suffering, the court said that her claim was based both on an implied covenant in the contract of insurance, as a matter of the law of contracts, and on the defendant's negligent conduct, as a matter of the law of torts. There are frequent border crossings between contract and torts.

† Except for convenience, the rubrics are not as such part of the law, although at one time they might have been so regarded, because they determined the "forms of action," procedural requirements for cases of one kind or another. See F. W. Maitland, *The Forms of Action at Common Law* (1936). The rubrics themselves are as likely to be determined by some external consideration, like

Legal Reason

the focus is sharpened, more and more facts are included –
a person's loss of property... while reposing confidence in
another... without the other's negligence or fault... on a
steamboat... that provides overnight lodging... – and the
rule is drawn more and more narrowly, until there emerges
a rule that uniquely applies to those facts.

At some point, the convergence of law and facts comes
to an end. However comprehensively the wording of a rule
specifies the circumstances in which it is to be applied, it cannot specify *all* the facts of a particular concrete case without
losing the quality of a rule.* Inevitably, if words are to com-
municate at all beyond merely pointing to something that is
immediately present ("Not this, that!"), they are more or less
general. No words fully exhaust the description of what they
describe – fully replicate, as it were, the thing itself – and,
therefore, they cannot wholly eliminate the possibility of further specification by the inclusion of some additional qualification – "When I said that you could buy a book, I didn't

the law school curriculum or the scope of a treatise or restatement, as by a real
boundary between one area of conduct and another.
* "There are no rules for particulars." Frederick Schauer, *Playing by the Rules* 17
(1991). That is why, when a court wants to overrule a prior case without quite
saying so, it declares that the rule of that case is "limited to its own facts," as
the Supreme Court said of *Jewell-LaSalle* in *Fortnightly*. See p. 50. For another
example, see *Kirby v. Illinois*, 406 U.S. 682, 689 (1972), in which the Court, having
changed its mind about the constitutional basis for limits on police interrogation
of suspects, see *Miranda v. Arizona*, 384 U.S. 436, 465–466 (1966), declared that
its holding two years earlier in *Escobedo v. Illinois*, 378 U.S. 478 (1964), was
"limited . . . to its own facts."

rules of law that favor his client's position and, so far as the rules permit, will *interpret* them in a manner that supports that position. Adjusting the characterization of the facts and the interpretation of the law mutually to one another, the lawyer's objective is to weave the two together into a coherent account pointing to the conclusion that the law applied to those facts dictates but one outcome. The opposing lawyer will make the same effort in the same manner, but she will, of course, direct her argument toward a different outcome.

In *Adams*, there was no rule that expressly defined the liability of steamboat operators, and the general rule was that a person is not liable for another person's loss unless it is due to the former's negligence. Innkeepers were subject to a stricter rule, which made them liable as an insurer, that is, without proof of negligence, for their guests' losses. It was, therefore, in the interest of the plaintiff to emphasize that the steamboat on which Adams took passage provided overnight lodging, like an inn, and to disregard the fact that it was not a building at all but a means of transportation that went up and down river, as an inn certainly does not. Bringing the facts to the rule, as it were, was evidently easier than bringing the rule to the facts and arguing directly that the rule about an innkeeper's liability was intended and should be understood to refer not only to innkeepers but also to the operator of a steamboat carrying passengers upriver overnight. Whichever the argument, the outcome that it supported, which the plaintiff favored, was the same. The defendant's lawyers, on the other hand, would have emphasized the difference between an inn, stationary on land, and a steamboat traveling upriver and the similarity between the latter and a railroad sleeping car, an operator of which was not subject to the stricter liability rule.

In its opinion, the court adopted the plaintiff's characterization of the steamboat and called it "for all practical purposes, a floating inn," "one of the modern floating palaces that...navigate the interior waters of the country."[1] With that analogy in place, the rule about an innkeeper's liability became applicable and the rule about the liability of the operator of a railroad sleeping car, which might have been thought relevant, became inapt. At the same time, the court made a nod in the direction of the plaintiff's alternative argument. If the innkeepers' rule did not apply in terms to steamboat operators, still "the same considerations of public policy apply."[2]

Similarly, in *Katz*, considering the electronic eavesdropping of Katz's telephone conversation and confronted by the rule of *Olmstead* that a search and seizure under the Fourth Amendment involves a trespass, the Court might have taken either of two routes toward its holding that the eavesdropping was a violation of his constitutional right. It might have relied on a factual analogy and declared that the eavesdropping was a trespass (or was "constructively" a trespass or was a "quasi-trespass"*), thus bringing the facts of the case within the rule of *Olmstead*, or it might have declared, as it did, that a search and seizure under the Fourth Amendment does not necessarily include a physical trespass, thereby expanding the rule to embrace the facts. Just six years earlier, in another case not so unlike *Katz*, the Court had adopted the former rationale.[3] Police officers gained access to a vacant row house adjoining premises that they believed were used as headquarters for an illegal gambling operation. By means of a "spike mike" inserted into the common wall between the houses, which came in contact with a heating duct of the suspect house, they were able to overhear conversations that took place there. Distinguishing another case in which the Court had held that attaching a listening device to a common wall without penetrating it did *not* constitute a search and seizure,[4] the Court emphasized that the spike mike had been stuck *into* the wall and, reasoning analogically, concluded that this "unauthorized physical penetration into the premises" occupied by the defendants satisfied the trespass requirement of a search and seizure "whether or not there was a technical trespass under the local property law."[5] In a concurring opinion, Justice Douglas objected to the Court's rationale, which, he argued, made such cases depend

---

* "Constructively" and "quasi-" mean roughly "might as well have been."

on a triviality – "the depth of the penetration of the electronic device" – rather than the invasion of privacy, which was the same whatever kind of electronic equipment was employed.[6] In *Katz*, mindful of the result in the earlier case, the federal agents who put the eavesdropping device in place had not penetrated the wall of the telephone booth;[7] so if anything remained of the requirement of a trespass, the eavesdropping could not easily have been described as a search and seizure. Instead, following Justice Douglas's line of reasoning, the Court modified the rule and enlarged the meaning of "search and seizure" to include eavesdropping without any physical intrusion in the circumstances of that case.[*][8]

Having the facts of a case before him and looking within the body of the law for a ground of decision, the task of the lawyer or judge is first to locate the facts within a broad area

---

[*] Bringing the facts within the rule has its limits. There is a well-known anecdote about a dean of Worcester College at Oxford University, who lived on the grounds of the college and kept a dog named Flint in his rooms. Someone was said to have objected, because a university regulation excluded dogs from college grounds. According to the story, the dean responded, "Sir, my dog is a cat." See John Walsh, "Harry's Dogs," in Lesley Le Claire, *For Harry* 54, 57–58 (Abbey Press, Abingdon 2001). The dog remained in the dean's rooms; but one may believe that the dean's reply stretched the limits of language and its interpretation to – or beyond – the breaking point. The strict classification of animal species makes it difficult, without tongue in cheek, to urge that a dog is a cat; but if Flint had been a good mouser, who knows? The dean's response would have been less remarkable if, instead of characterizing the facts to make his point, he had interpreted the law and said, in the manner of a legal argument, that despite the unqualified language of the regulation, it was not intended to apply to college officers or to the dean, or that the prohibition against dogs did not include very small dogs or dogs that are well-behaved.

of the law dealing with that kind of human conduct, and then, including more and more particular detail, progressively to sharpen the focus until there emerges a rule that applies squarely to those facts. Ordinarily, the relevant area of the law is quickly and easily determined, because the categories of the law correspond, as they must, to the kinds of controversies that arise. Occasionally, the facts of a case do not lie neatly within one clearly defined category or another but fall on the border between two well-defined categories, so that rules of law from both may alike have some bearing on the outcome.* The familiar legal categories – torts, contract, criminal law, environmental law, securities regulation, and so forth – are, in any event, not rigid and mutually exclusive but are rather conventional rubrics that refer to a grouping of rules related together by the kind of conduct with which they deal.† As

---

* See, for example, *Crisci v. Security Insurance Co. of New Haven, Conn.*, 426 P.2d 173 (Cal. 1967), in which the plaintiff, who suffered a large judgment against her in a personal injury action, sued the defendant, her insurer, for refusing to settle the claim at a much lower figure, within the amount of the insurance policy. The plaintiff claimed damages including an amount for mental suffering. Upholding an award of damages to the plaintiff that included compensation for the amount of the judgment against her and for her mental suffering, the court said that her claim was based both on an implied covenant in the contract of insurance, as a matter of the law of contracts, and on the defendant's negligent conduct, as a matter of the law of torts. There are frequent border crossings between contract and torts.

† Except for convenience, the rubrics are not as such part of the law, although at one time they might have been so regarded, because they determined the "forms of action," procedural requirements for cases of one kind or another. See F. W. Maitland, *The Forms of Action at Common Law* (1936). The rubrics themselves are as likely to be determined by some external consideration, like

the focus is sharpened, more and more facts are included –
a person's loss of property... while reposing confidence in
another... without the other's negligence or fault... on a
steamboat... that provides overnight lodging... – and the
rule is drawn more and more narrowly, until there emerges
a rule that uniquely applies to those facts.

At some point, the convergence of law and facts comes
to an end. However comprehensively the wording of a rule
specifies the circumstances in which it is to be applied, it cannot specify *all* the facts of a particular concrete case without
losing the quality of a rule.* Inevitably, if words are to com-
municate at all beyond merely pointing to something that is
immediately present ("Not this, that!"), they are more or less
general. No words fully exhaust the description of what they
describe – fully replicate, as it were, the thing itself – and,
therefore, they cannot wholly eliminate the possibility of further specification by the inclusion of some additional qualification – "When I said that you could buy a book, I didn't

the law school curriculum or the scope of a treatise or restatement, as by a real
boundary between one area of conduct and another.
* "There are no rules for particulars." Frederick Schauer, *Playing by the Rules* 17
(1991). That is why, when a court wants to overrule a prior case without quite
saying so, it declares that the rule of that case is "limited to its own facts," as
the Supreme Court said of *Jewell-LaSalle* in *Fortnightly*. See p. 50. For another
example, see *Kirby v. Illinois*, 406 U.S. 682, 689 (1972), in which the Court, having
changed its mind about the constitutional basis for limits on police interrogation
of suspects, see *Miranda v. Arizona*, 384 U.S. 436, 465–466 (1966), declared that
its holding two years earlier in *Escobedo v. Illinois*, 378 U.S. 478 (1964), was
"limited . . . to its own facts."

mean a comic book" – or by the exclusion of some qualification that had been implicitly taken for granted – "When I
said that you could buy a book, I didn't mean that it had to
be an educational one." The explicit use of comprehensive
quantifiers ("any," "all," "no") makes the addition or elimination of further qualifications problematic and, no doubt, less
convincing; but so long as the qualification is rendered as part
of the meaning of the words themselves and not as a departure
from them, it cannot be barred altogether – "When I said 'any
book,' I certainly did not mean a *comic book*!" Furthermore,
although the words that we use to describe our experience are
cast as discrete categories, the actual phenomena are mostly
continuous; "nature" and, generally, human contrivances as
well avoid sharp breaks. Some general categories leave little
room for uncertainty ("all men at least eighteen years old");
but there is typically, for the most part unavoidably, a range
of uncertainty at the boundaries, in which some phenomena
will fall.* For both reasons – because words, as symbols with

---

* Even "men eighteen years old" is not without ambiguity. See *Parker v. State*, 484
A.2d 1020 (Md. App. 1984), in which the defendant argued that he was not tri-
able as an adult because he was not eighteen years old at the time of the offense
charged against him; the offense was committed on his eighteenth birthday at
9:45 A.M., and he was born at 12:50 P.M. Referring back to an English case decided
in 1663, the court rejected the argument. The incertitude can be eliminated by
enumerating all the members of a closed category ("John, Jane, and Janet Jones")
rather than naming the category itself ("the children of James Jones whenever
born"); but that would deprive the proposition in question of the generality required of a rule. (If James Jones were an eighty-year-old widower, one might
suppose that the category of "the children of James Jones" was effectively closed.

meaning, are general and phenomena, as such, are particular, and because words, however precise, do not fully distinguish phenomena in all their variety – there remains a gap between a rule and its applications that no further statement of the rule or specification of the facts will close completely. Any rule that otherwise appears to apply to the facts of a case will be silent about some of its concrete details. One or another such detail – the steamboat's mobility or its provision of lodging, the absence of physical trespass or the intrusion on a private conversation – may appear to be of special significance or to be manifestly irrelevant, according to the content of the rule under consideration. But none can be disregarded or declared to be irrelevant out of hand, because it is that case and no other that is to be decided.

Having thus to bridge the gap between facts and rule, one may refer to some rule of decision, itself part of the law, that provides how much weight should be given to facts, or factors, of one kind or another or which of two conflicting rules should prevail. Such a rule also is general in form, and

But the category is general, and incertitude remains: for example, whether a child whom he later adopts or the stepchildren of the widow whom he later marries are included.)

For a well-known discussion of this problem in relation to law, which distinguishes between a general term's "core of settled meaning" and "a penumbra of debatable cases in which words are neither obviously applicable nor obviously ruled out," see H.L.A. Hart, *Positivism and the Separation of Law and Morals,* 71 Harv. L. Rev. 593, 607 (1958), and Lon L. Fuller, *Positivism and Fidelity to Law – A Reply to Professor Hart,* 71 Harv. L. Rev. 630, 661–669 (1958).

there will remain a gap between it and the particular occasions of its application.* In short, at some point in the argument, the content of the rules themselves runs out, and straightforward application of the law to the facts will falter. Having to take account of all the facts in their unique detail and having to lodge them under a rule of law, the lawyer or judge will have recourse to analogical reasoning to decide whether, all things considered, the facts more closely resemble facts subsumed under one rule or under another, actually or hypothetically.

Although no rule dictates a decision, in the manner of a deductive argument, the choice of which analogy to prefer is not like a flip of the coin. Just as her common sense, the accumulation of ordinary experience, tells Edna that it makes no difference how much cranberry juice costs or whether it is imported, a lawyer or judge relies on his knowledge and experience of the law. The greater his expertise in the particular area of the law, the more likely it is that the analogy he chooses will be convincing to others (just as Edna's

---

* "Particular fact-situations do not await us already marked off from each other, and labeled as instances of the general rule, the application of which is in question; nor can the rule itself step forward to claim its own instances. . . . Canons of 'interpretation' cannot eliminate, though they can diminish, these uncertainties; for these canons are themselves general rules for the use of language, and make use of general terms which themselves require interpretation. They cannot, any more than other rules, provide for their own interpretation." H.L.A. Hart, *The Concept of Law* 126 (2d ed. 1994).

advice to Mary would be more convincing if she had a degree in food chemistry). The choice is informed also by a broad understanding of what is relevant to the sort of decision being made – a matter of liability (*Adams*) or regulation of business (*Jewell-LaSalle*) or individual rights (*Katz*) – and, broader still, what generally "counts" in the law. Especially when the choice is a close one – as able lawyers in a seriously contested case will make it appear to be – the lawyers' grasp of the issues may be attributed to nothing more definite than "intuition," and the judge's decision to a "hunch" or "whim." But it is the law itself (as well, of course, as ordinary common sense) on which a decision properly rests and on the basis of which, carefully articulated, it commands assent. A decision is not a proof; it does not afford certainty, and reasonable persons may disagree. But in law, as in human affairs generally, a proof is not to be had.

Surely, however, there are judicial opinions in which analogical argument is absent or plays a subordinate role. The need for and the prominence of analogical argument is directly related to the size of the gap between facts and rule that such argument serves to fill. If the facts of a case are, as it is said, "on all fours" with the facts of a prior case and fall squarely under the rule of that case, there is little need to engage explicitly in analogical reasoning, for the conjunction of facts and rule is accomplished without it. Had Adams spent the night at an inn, instead of on a steamboat, the innkeeper's liability would have been clear, and the case would probably not have been appealed on that ground to two higher courts. So also, had the government agents eavesdropped on Katz's telephone call by means of a "spike mike," as in the earlier case, it would not have required more than a citation to that case to vindicate his claim.* Sometimes, although there is not a prior case precisely on point, the court or another superior court has nevertheless indicated in an opinion how a case like that should be decided. Discussing the liability of an innkeeper in some prior case, for example, the New York Court of Appeals might have observed that "innkeepers *and all others who provide private accommodations overnight on land or water* are liable as insurers for their guest's losses." Had it done so, the court in *Adams* could have relied directly on that and would

---

* Even when a case is on all fours with a prior case, an element of analogical reasoning is necessary. For no two cases are alike in *all* respects, and a rule cannot dispositively determine its own application, any provision about its range of application having itself to be interpreted. One might say, therefore, that strictly speaking, analogical reasoning is needed to connect the rule of the earlier case to the particular facts of the later one. The similarity between the facts of the two cases being so strong, however, and the dissimilarities so obviously irrelevant, there is no need to make the analogy explicit. In such a case, the process of thought more closely resembles the ordinary use of general terms, which we are able to extend easily and uncontroversially to particular instances not precisely similar to anything that we have seen before. The capacity for analogical reasoning is inherent in our ability to use general terms. See pp. 124–130.

not have needed to draw the analogy between innkeepers and operators of steamboats.*

Sometimes also, in the absence of a rule that plainly covers the facts of a case, a court formulates a covering rule on the basis of instrumental arguments that do not as such depend on analogical reasoning. So, in *Adams*, the court observed that passengers on a steamboat ought to be protected against the opportunities for theft. Likewise, in *Katz*, the Court called attention to the reasonable expectation of privacy of a person in a telephone booth. In both cases, the court evidently believed that the effects of its decision would be salutary. However weighty such an argument might have been as a straightforward matter of public policy, it would have been entitled to no weight in the case before the court, without the support of analogical reasoning. For the case was to be decided according to the law, and whatever instrumental arguments the court brought to bear had to be found finally within the law itself. The argument that it was sound policy to protect passengers on a steamboat from theft had a foothold in *Adams*

---

* Since, presumably, the defendant in the earlier case *was* an innkeeper, however, the court's observation about those who provide accommodations on water would have been dictum, because it was not necessary to the decision. Courts sometimes observe that dictum is not binding in a later case. See, e.g., *Harris v. New York*, 401 U.S. 222, 224 (1971), rejecting as dictum some of the Court's opinion five years earlier in *Miranda v. Arizona*, 384 U.S. 436 (1966). But the distinction between a holding and dictum is not always clear and, in any event, if it is the same court in both cases (and its membership has not changed) it is likely to treat all its words with respect.

because a steamboat was a "floating inn," and that argument had been used to justify the rule about innkeepers. In *Katz*, the expectation of privacy of a person in a telephone booth made a difference, because it was analogous to the expectation of a person "in a business office, in a friend's apartment, or in a taxicab," which the Fourth Amendment had previously been held to protect. The opinions in *Adams* and *Katz* would have been very different and would have been subject to criticism had there been no such analogical connection to prior law and the court had relied simply on its conclusion that the outcome that it reached was desirable. At a more general level as well, when a judge relies on one type of argument – authoritative text or public policy or some more general consideration – rather than another, he may draw an analogy to prior cases in quite different areas of the law, to show that such reliance is legally grounded and not *ad hoc*.

The judge is thus in a different situation from that of Edna and Charlie, who are under no general constraint about how to solve the problems before them, except that the solution be effective. Although they are likely to reason by analogy, they need not. They might experiment with different solutions until they find one that works (although they will almost certainly rely on analogical reasoning to narrow the range of their experiments). Or they might refer to a rule that covers the case, which might come from any source whatever. If Edna had not herself removed any stains in the past, she might find no basis in her own experience from which to draw an analogy. (She might, of course, lacking an alternative, draw an analogy, however dubious, from a more remote source: washing clothes or washing dishes or washing the dog.) Instead, recalling that her Aunt Lizzie had once told her that salt removes lots of stains, she might rely simply on that. Or she might refer to a rule, again from any source – "My Aunt Lizzie told me that salt removes wine stains" – and use analogical reasoning to extend it to Mary's particular problem. Of course, the more reliable the source of such a rule, the more likely Mary is to take Edna's advice. Similarly, if Charlie's neighbor likes to work on small engines, Charlie might just ask him to get his lawn mower started, while he watches television. A judge is not free to consider Aunt Lizzie's view, no matter how sensible she usually is – not, at least, unless she is an expert in that area of the law and has made her view public – nor may he ask his neighbor how to decide a case. For him, having to bring the facts of a case within a rule, analogical reasoning is not a convenience but a necessity.

There is no fixed order of precedence between an analogical argument that supports the application of a rule and the reasons for the rule that are then mustered in support of its application. Which precedes and prompts the other is not a logical question but an epistemic one, the answer to which varies from one judge to another and from case to case; very likely the analogy and the instrumental arguments that support it will be considered together. The reasons for a rule may support the analogy, because, as in *Adams* and *Katz*, they apply alike to the source and the target and thus help to establish that the similarity on which the analogy depends is relevant. At the same time, the analogy legitimates reference to the reasons underlying the rule as within the purview of the court. One or the other may carry the greater weight. For if the reasons for a rule are not substantial, that may suggest that the analogy supporting its application is weak and that some other analogy pointing to a different rule is to be preferred. Or, if the analogy is weak, that may suggest that less weight should be given to the reasons for the rule to which the analogy points. As a general matter, the stronger the reasons for a rule, the less compelling the similarity between source and target needs to be to sustain the analogy, and the more compelling the similarity, the weaker the reasons may be without making the analogy irrelevant.

In sum, however strong a judge's personal convictions – whatever their source – about the matter, she is not at liberty to decide a case as she thinks is right or best, all things considered. She may not engage in social or economic engineering at large. For, as the Supreme Court repeatedly acknowledged in the cable transmission cases, means as well as ends are for the legislature to determine. Rather, applying analogical reasoning to the details that give a case its novelty, the judge must bring the case within a rule – if not a rule about overnight passengers on steamboats, then a rule about guests in public accommodations or, still more generally, a rule about liability for injury to others. At some level of generality, the facts of the case will no longer be unique, and, making an analogical connection to the facts of another case, she will have a basis for decision according to the law. Of course, as particular facts are disregarded and the description becomes more general, not only one but several rules are likely to be more or less on point, and the judge will have to choose, by analogical reasoning, which is most nearly applicable.

Courts sometimes speak of a case as a "case of first impression," meaning that no similar case has previously been decided. Just as there is not a sharp line that separates a case "on all fours" from cases that are just more or less similar, there is not a sharp line between a case of first impression and other cases. No case is wholly unlike prior cases; there are always similarities, which can be emphasized or passed over. If, examined up close, two cases seem to be very different, from a more distant perspective, the details fade and a more general similarity appears. Considered as a case involving the liability of a steamship operator for an overnight passenger's loss, *Adams* was a case of first impression. Considered as a case involving the liability of persons who provide sleeping accommodations for travelers, it was, according to the court, if not on all fours with the innkeeper cases, very similar – analogous – to them and dissimilar to the railroad sleeping car cases. Had there been no special rule for innkeepers or had the court not been persuaded by the analogy between innkeepers and steamboat operators, no narrower analogy being available, the court would have considered the facts from a still more distant perspective and, presumably, found a similarity to cases in the fully general category of liability for another person's loss. Insofar as it involved a wiretap without any physical trespass of a conversation made from a public telephone booth, *Katz* was a case of first impression. Nevertheless, the Court found that there was significant similarity to cases that involved a business office, a friend's apartment, or a taxicab, not to mention *Olmstead*, which was so closely on point (despite any number of differences) that the Court was obliged to overrule it.

The same is true in the small number of cases in which a court turns its back on a rule that appears clearly to be applicable and declares a contrary rule. Whatever differences there may be between the facts of the present case and the facts of prior cases in which the existing rule was applied, they are deemed too slight to permit a difference in result, and the court announces another rule that attaches new and different significance to those facts. The Supreme Court's decision in *Fortnightly* effectively, if not in so many words, overruled its decision thirty-seven years earlier in *Jewell-LaSalle* that the reception and transmission of a radio broadcast was a "performance" within the meaning of the Copyright Act. The later case involved television, not radio; nonetheless, the Court regarded the facts of the cases as too similar for it to hold that the reception and transmission of a television broadcast is *not* a performance without applying its revised analysis to radio as well. Sometimes, albeit rarely, a court undertakes to review a long line of prior decisions that have cohered in settled rules and to reconsider an entire rubric of the law. Such cases not only overrule past decisions precisely on point; the reasoning expressed in the court's opinion may radiate more broadly and generate revisions in the law that affect cases involving quite different issues.* The decision in *Katz* was such a landmark. Discarding the requirement of a trespass, on which it had relied in *Olmstead*, and replacing it with the notion of a

---

* The best-known constitutional decision of this kind is *Brown v. Board of Education of Topeka*, 347 U.S. 483 (1954), in which the Court declared that the "separate but equal" doctrine *of Plessy v. Ferguson*, 163 U.S. 537 (1896), has no place in public education. *Brown* set the law on a new course not only in the field of public education but also with respect to racial discrimination generally. A well-known example of such a landmark decision in American common law *is MacPherson v. Buick Motor Co.*, 111 N.E. 1050 (N.Y. 1916), in which the court greatly expanded the liability of the seller of a dangerous article for injury to someone other than the purchaser. For one among many discussions of *MacPherson*, see Edward H. Levi, *An Introduction to Legal Reasoning* 20–25 (1949).

"legitimate expectation of privacy" as the core of the Fourth Amendment, the Court prompted reconsideration of issues that had little directly to do with eavesdropping on telephone conversations.* On the other hand, even after being overruled, some residue of prior decisions may remain, especially if they have become doctrinally embedded. After the decision in *Katz*, the Supreme Court several times noted that although the element of trespass was no longer critical, whether an expectation of privacy is legitimate depends significantly on one's relations to the premises where the invasion of privacy occurs.[9]

Whether its reach is narrow or broad, "overruling" is not like a wild card that a court is free to play, provided that it does not play the card too often. Rather, it occurs because a court concludes that the rule that was previously in place is inconsistent with some other rule of more general application and that, both appearing to be applicable to the particular facts, the former must give way. In effect, the court concludes that facts that had been thought to distinguish a case of that kind and to warrant a distinct rule do not do so and, therefore, that the more general rule applies. On rare occasions, a court may overrule a relatively narrow rule simply because it has

---

* In *Rakas v. Illinois*, 439 U.S. 128 (1978), for example, the Supreme Court reconsidered the question of standing – who is entitled – to assert a violation of the Fourth Amendment as a ground for the suppression of evidence in a criminal case. It abandoned a rule that had roots in the trespass rationale of *Olmstead* and substituted a rule that made a "legitimate expectation of privacy" critical.

proved to be unworkable or to have unforeseen consequences. The instrumental aspect of such a decision is evident; but it does not eliminate the requirement that the new rule not be inconsistent with other rules that prevail over it.* The law is, in a sense, a "seamless web," not because it prescribes in advance the outcome of every case that may arise, but because when a case does arise, however unusual it may be, the outcome is to be found within the law.

The pattern of legal reasoning described above is only that, a pattern, which allows considerable variation in detail. Lawyers and judges have individual rhetorical styles, which are reflected in briefs and oral arguments and in judicial opinions. Someone who follows the workings of an appellate court may be able to identify the author of an opinion from its style, even though it is written to reflect the views of other members of the court as well. Individual differences aside, the pattern of reasoning generally changes as a case advances from the trial court to an intermediate appellate court and from there

---

* See, e.g., *California v. Acevedo*, 500 U.S. 565 (1991), in which the Court revised the rules about when police officers can, without a search warrant, search a piece of luggage or a similar container found in a car. Making strict inferences from two distinct lines of prior cases, the Court had previously stated complex rules that depended on whether the police had probable cause to believe that the item to be seized was in the container itself or simply somewhere in the car. Concluding that the rules were difficult to apply and to enforce and added little to the protection of privacy, the Court substituted a rule that applied uniformly in both situations. It acknowledged that it was making the change because the prior rules were confusing, but it asserted that despite their stricter logic, the uniform rule was no less consistent with the values of the Fourth Amendment.

to the highest court of the jurisdiction, which has final judicial authority. A trial judge, having primary responsibility to determine the facts and subject to appellate review on matters of law, is likely to stay close to the higher courts' statements of the law. He lacks authority to overrule a decision of a higher court and rarely will rely on a distinction of fact that has no foundation in a higher court's reasoning. An appellate court, on the other hand, relying for matters of fact on the findings below, exercises more independent judgment about the law and its correct application to the facts. It is freer to look beyond the area of the law that is immediately at stake and to reconsider the applicable rule in light of more general rules and rules drawn from other contexts. The highest court has the greatest freedom in this respect. It is less likely to regard its own decisions as indicative of a settled rule and more likely to find room for an interpretation that is not clearly signaled. But throughout, the task remains the same: to apply the law as it is, however narrowly or broadly conceived, to the concrete facts of the case, in all their particularity.

c. The hierarchy of rules

If now we return to the model of legal reasoning as a hierarchy of rules, it can be seen more clearly why it is inadequate. Being

[103]

concerned entirely with rules and their relationship with one another and having no place for analogical argument, the model lacks means for deciding a concrete case. The rules have reciprocal effect, but the achievement of consistency among them is empty, because no method is given or allowed for attaching one rule or another to the facts of a case. If a case closely resembles another case in which a rule was declared, the lack of attachment between the rule and the facts of the later case may be overlooked, on the basis of the similarity. As the cases discussed in Chapter Two illustrate, however, in a seriously contested case, more than one rule is claimed to be applicable, which may be consistent among themselves and have a place within the hierarchy of rules. At that point, the rules themselves are inert and require an analogical argument to bring the reasoning to closure.

Although those who defend the model of law as a hierarchy of rules forcefully reject the "mechanical jurisprudence" of classical legal theory of the nineteenth and early twentieth centuries,* they end up in the same place. It was the central tenet of classical theory that the law could be expressed as a formally complete deductive system. The need for analogical reasoning was recognized; but the deductive system was preserved by supposing that the analogical reach of a legal

* See pp. 139–140.

concept was determinate and that "analogical reasoning from similar cases or principles provided a self-executing process of discovery, at least for those learned in the law."[10] The error, even absurdity, of that position, essential as it was to maintenance of law as a deductive system, made it an easy target for the Legal Realists. Instead of asserting that analogical reasoning is fully determinate, the hierarchical model's exclusive focus on rules hides it from view; but no more than the classical theory does the model explain how, without analogical reasoning, an actual case is decided.

If this model is inadequate as a complete account of legal reasoning, it is not to be rejected altogether. Although rules unaided by analogical reasoning are powerless, it is true also that without a consistent, relatively stable body of rules, analogical reasoning would be aimless. (The same is true of analogical practical reasoning, which supposes that the causal properties of things being compared are stable, even if the physical processes are unknown.) For within a legal order, the body of rules provides the criteria of relevance that distinguish a good analogy from a bad one.* Were a court confronted with two inconsistent rules derived from prior cases that resembled the case before the court in just the same way, analogical reasoning

---

* That is not to say that an analogy is in any sense deducible from the rules. See p. 138.

would not help the court to render a decision, unless the prior cases were first distinguished in some way that enabled the court, looking at the facts of the case before it, to choose between them. It is, therefore, a major part of the work of the law, carried on not only in the course of adjudication but in secondary activities like drafting restatements and writing treatises, to reconcile cases in the manner of the hierarchical model. If judges rarely undertake a full "justificatory ascent,"* nevertheless the process of reconciliation and systematization goes on piecemeal all the time and occasionally is embodied in a full statement that approximates the ideal model.

As cases dealing with a particular area of the law are decided, the rules dealing with topics within that area are elaborated in greater detail, some distinctions being approved and embodied in rules and others being asserted and, after consideration, rejected. The demand for consistency leads in time to the formulation of general principles that account for the distinctions that are made. One might, then, suppose that analogical reasoning is essential for application of a body of law when it is young but dispensable once it has matured and broad general principles encompassing more particular rules and distinctions have been articulated. It has been suggested that natural science develops in much that way and that the

---

* See p. 7.

displacement of analogical reasoning by explanatory principles is the mark of a mature science.[11] Although cases would continue to arise, they would mostly be settled on the facts, without explicit analogical argument. Some such movement in that direction does occur. But it is a matter of more or less, not the elimination of analogical reasoning altogether. The endless variability of the familiar, accompanied by discoveries in the natural sciences, development of new technologies, and changes in the political and social context, presents issues that have not been seen before, which call for new distinctions or revisions of distinctions that had previously been made. The rationalization of the law is a continuing process, which does not achieve the clarity and stability of a deductive system. Human motivation and experience are too protean for that.

d. Objections

The variety of scholarly responses to the central role of analogical arguments in legal reasoning has been noted. They range from approval for instrumental political reasons, qualified by a concession that such arguments are logically defective,* to

---

* E.g., Levi and Sunstein.

simple disapproval because they do not address important instrumental issues* and, most common of all, dismissal as a disguised deductive argument and not a distinct form of reasoning at all.[†] Scarcely any of them regards analogical arguments as what they purport to be: arguments valid on their own terms. For all that, lawyers and judges rely on them routinely and display no doubt about their merit, although, of course, they do their best to defend their own analogical arguments and question those on the other side.

There is more common ground among those who disparage analogical legal arguments than immediately appears. Collateral political benefits or instrumental deficiencies aside, they share a belief that what appears to be reasoning by analogy, inferring one similarity from another, should be analyzed as if it were something else: a deductive inference, preceded, perhaps, by an inductive step to frame the general rule on which the inference depends. And if it is not that, they assert, it does not properly qualify as reasoning at all and is as likely to be wrong as right. The difficulty is not that we are unable to perceive similarities between one thing or event or circumstance and another: between wine and cranberry juice, or an inn and a steamboat. On the contrary, it is that we can and do perceive such similarities, as well as dissimilarities – all too

* E.g., Posner and, apparently, Brewer.
[†] E.g., Alexander et al., p. 11n.

many of them. There are numberless similarities between one concrete entity and another of the same general kind.* And nothing in the similarities themselves links one similarity (or group of similarities) to any other in the manner that an analogy requires. On the face of it, instead of supposing that if salt removes a wine stain, it will probably also remove a cranberry juice stain, one might as easily suppose that, both being red, drinking too much cranberry juice will make you drunk, or that salt and talcum powder both being white, a pinch of talcum powder will improve the taste of the soup. Instead of reasoning that since a steamboat that provides overnight lodging is entrusted with a person's goods in circumstances similar to those of an inn, its operator should be similarly liable for the person's loss, one might as easily reason that since a steamboat and a railroad sleeping car both transport passengers, the operator of one should be no more liable than the operator of the other. One can take the step from one similarity to another only if the former is relevant as an explanation, or at least an indicator of the explanation, of the latter. So, it is argued, in order for an analogy to succeed, there must be about somewhere, if not explicitly then implicitly, if not consciously then unawares, a general rule that applies to both things being

---

* If two entities are of entirely different kinds – a day of the week and a pig – it may be difficult to perceive any similarities between them. Metaphors, which suggest unusual similarities, have power just because they elude the usual categories.

compared and provides that all members of a class to which both belong (signaled, perhaps, by the observed similarity between them) have the further characteristic that is in doubt.

Peter Westen states the position clearly:

> One can never declare A to be legally similar to B without first formulating the legal rule of treatment by which they are rendered relevantly identical.... Before one has identified the prevailing legal rule, one has no way of knowing whether the acts are legally similar or dissimilar. After one has identified the prevailing rule, the similarities or dissimilarities of the two acts follow as a logical consequence: their similarity or dissimilarity... is simply another way of saying that they either do or do not both fully satisfy the terms of the prevailing rule.[12]

Westen refers specifically to legal similarity, but his point is more general. It is, he argues, meaningless to say that one thing is similar to another abstractly, without identifying a ground that indicates which among their innumerable similarities and dissimilarities "count." If the provision of separate sleeping accommodations is what counts, a steamboat with guest cabins is similar to an inn; if being a means of transportation is what counts, a steamboat is similar to a railroad car; and if emitting steam is what counts, a steamboat is similar to a tea kettle. In a great many ordinary circumstances, the specification is obvious or taken for granted and need not be stated expressly; but some such indication must be contained in or implied by a declaration that two things are similar, to establish the relevance of the particular similarities (and irrelevance of the dissimilarities) at stake. It is perhaps not clear whether Westen means to describe the mental process of a person who makes such a declaration or the declaration itself. It is evident, at any rate, that most analogies are made without express reference to a rule of the kind that he indicates. But it makes no difference which he has in mind. For neither in the actual process of analogical reasoning nor in a reconstruction of the analogy is such a rule ordinarily to be found.

In *Adams*, what legal rule dictated that the operator of a steamboat be regarded as analogous to an innkeeper, with respect to liability for a passenger's loss? There are, as the court noted, similarities between them, notably the confidence that a lodger or passenger places in them and the temptation to fraud. There are also many dissimilarities, including most obviously, the fact that an inn is on land and provides lodging and a steamboat is on water and is a means of transportation. No rule definitively sorted those similarities and dissimilarities and all the others into those that were relevant and those that were not, although someone knowledgeable in the law might have speculated that the court would rule as it did. Nor can the court's reasoning be reconstructed as a deductive argument, with a "prevailing legal rule" from which the steamboat operator's liability can be deduced. Having the rule about an innkeeper's liability (as well, of course, as a rule about an operator of a railroad sleeping car and any number of other rules), how does one arrive at a rule about the liability of a steamboat operator? That, of course, is the work of the analogy – a steamboat is a "floating inn" – which is not rendered unnecessary by recasting the argument in deductive form.* Nor, after the decision in *Adams*, can one confidently refer to a prevailing rule broader than the decision itself, without relying on analogical reasoning. For in subsequent cases, a court might deem relevant some similarity or dissimilarity that the *Adams* court passed by – say, the fact that the steamboat in question provides sleeping berths and not staterooms – and come up with a different result – that the steamboat was less like an inn than a railroad sleeping car and the rule about the latter should apply.

Similarly, in *Katz*, although the Court indicated that it did not matter whether there was a trespass and that Katz's legitimate expectation of privacy in the telephone booth sustained his rights under the Fourth Amendment, as it would

---

* Westen's reference to "the prevailing legal rule," without saying how it is determined which legal rule prevails, begs the question. If a steamboat is (analogous to) an inn, then one legal rule prevails. If it is (analogous to) a railroad sleeping car, then another rule prevails. And if it is neither, there is a third rule. Nor can the prevailing rule simply mirror *all* the characteristics of the particular case, which would deprive it of the quality of a rule.

in a business office, a friend's apartment, or a taxicab, there was no rule before *Katz* was decided that dictated that result, although those other cases might have led one to speculate in that direction. Nor, after *Katz* was decided, was there any certain rule broader than the terms of the analogy itself that followed from the decision. If lawyers and others referred to a "legitimate expectation of privacy" as the critical element in Fourth Amendment cases, that was not a firm rule but a speculative, imprecise generalization, as subsequent cases, presenting other similarities and differences, made clear. Although it might have been thought that, as a matter of fact, a person has a legitimate expectation of privacy and, therefore, a protected Fourth Amendment interest in a friend's automobile or apartment, in an enclosed yard surrounded by a high fence, or in a sealed trash bag placed at the curb for collection, it turned out that in some circumstances that was not so, anything to the contrary that the Court had seemed to say in *Katz* notwithstanding.[13]

The attempted reconstruction of analogical reasoning as a deductive argument fails also on another ground: it proves too much. By the same reasoning that would require a rule that makes the similarity on which an analogy rests relevant, so also would there have to be a rule for each and every one of the innumerable other similarities and dissimilarities between the two things being compared. Otherwise, how would one know that beside the similarity to which the rule referred, there was not some other feature of one or both that also was relevant to the outcome, which would be changed accordingly?* In *Adams*, on what basis could the court have concluded that the reason why innkeepers and operators of steamboats are similarly liable has to do with the confidence that lodgers/passengers repose in them and the temptation to fraud, rather than something else, like the fact that both serve meals (meaning that a boat that served no meals would not be similarly liable), or that it made no difference that an inn is stationary and a steamboat is not? Were those and every other comparison that might be made between inns and steamboats embodied in a "prevailing legal rule"? The suggestion refutes itself. The court's argument is nevertheless comprehensible and persuasive (even if it is not demonstrably true), because the analogy, in light of what we know about the law, makes it so.

Because a case is to be decided according to the law, it is easy to suppose that the "rule of the case," according to which

---

* "If the world in which we live were characterized only by a finite number of features, and these together with all the modes in which they could combine were known to us, then provision could be made in advance for every possibility. We could make rules, the application of which to particular cases never called for a further choice. Everything could be known, and for everything, since it could be known, something could be done and specified in advance by rule. This would be a world fit for 'mechanical' jurisprudence.

"Plainly, this world is not our world. . . ." Hart, *The Concept of Law*, p. 91n., at 128.

it is decided, must already have been part of the law. From that, it is not a large step to the proposition that the decision depends on the rule, and the further proposition that, as Westen says, the rule precedes and is essential to the validity of any analogy on which the decision rests. That, however, has the matter backwards. Although the materials – a statute and interpretations of it, prior decisions, and so forth – on the basis of which the case is decided are available beforehand, the rule of the case itself is not. The rule of the case is a generalized statement of the decision, not the predicate on which the decision rests. To be sure, once a case has been decided, the rule of the case is a part of the materials on which decisions *in future cases* are based (and, as such, is itself subject to interpretation). Rather than the analogy depending on the rule, the rule depends on the analogy, which is the means by which the materials of the law are brought to bear on the particular facts of that case.*

---

* "It is the merit of the common law that it decides the case first and determines the principle afterwards. Looking at the forms of logic it might be inferred that when you have a minor premise and a conclusion, there must be a major, which you are also prepared then and there to assert. But in fact lawyers, like other men, frequently see well enough how they ought to decide on a given state of facts without being very clear as to the *ratio decidendi*....It is only after a series of determinations on the same subject-matter, that it becomes necessary to 'reconcile the cases,' as it is called, that is, by a true induction to state the principle which has until then been obscurely felt." Oliver W. Holmes, Jr., *Codes, and the Arrangement of the Law*, 5 Am. L. Rev. 1, 1 (1870), reprinted in *The Early Writings of O. W. Holmes, Jr.*, 44 Harv. L. Rev. 717, 725 (1931).

In sum, Westen and others of the phantasm school suppose that the matter of relevance on which the weight of an analogy depends can be eliminated (and the analogy with it) by folding it into the statement of a general rule that applies deductively – "as a logical consequence" – to the facts at hand. The claim resembles the formalist belief that if the rules of a legal order are sufficiently articulated, the correct decision of a case can be found by deductive inference. It is not so. The elaboration of rules is an essential feature of adjudication, without which analogical reasoning would be without direction. It does not displace analogical reasoning but enables it to proceed according to the rule of law.

A different critical assessment of analogical legal arguments ignores their form and asserts that, except as they may aid in the elaboration of an inductive argument, they are useless and often worse than useless. Looking for similarities between cases, it is said, diverts attention from a court's proper concern, which is the practical consequences of a decision one way or the other. Although this criticism appears to address the substance of analogical arguments and not their form, its generality evidently depends on the assumption that they are formally inadequate and not simply badly reasoned in particular cases: Whether a rule is brought into the picture or not, the similarity between source and target does not bear the weight of the conclusion. They should, therefore, be replaced by empirically grounded, inductive arguments. So, Posner observes, with evident scorn:

> If [lawyers] have a case involving the appropriate system of property rights for a new natural resource, say petroleum, they examine decided cases dealing with "similar" resources, say water or rabbits. They do not go out and talk to petroleum engineers, ecologists, or natural-resources economists. They treat the issue as one *internal* to legal materials, an issue of the relations between legal concepts.*

He does not quite suggest that all that talk would be sufficient by itself; the judge has to "quarry" other cases (and presumably any relevant statutes) for the appropriate policies to pursue (a task that he apparently concedes involves reasoning by analogy).† Even so, taken at his word, he suggests that the decision should be reached empirically, without regard (at least with respect to how policy is implemented) to existing rules of law. But whether the issue is what policy to pursue or how

---

* Richard A. Posner, *Overcoming Law* 519 (1995). "[I]s it," he asks, "more than habit and indolence that causes lawyers and judges to look for the ethical and political materials of judgment in previous decisions rather than in scholarly literature, statistical compendia, and everyday experience?" Richard A. Posner, *The Problems of Jurisprudence* 94 (1990). Answering his own question, he says, "Well, it is a little more," insofar as the "blinkered vision" that results contributes to "greater stability in law." Id.

† Posner, *Overcoming Law*, above, at 518. Nevertheless, he deprecates such quarrying: "[L]aw is best regarded as a policy science – though maybe a primitive one, given its curious dependence on those policy considerations that can be culled from published judicial opinions...." Id. at 519.

to pursue it, a judge is not free to decide a case on that basis. All the talk in the world with engineers, ecologists, and even economists is beside the point unless what they have to say is reflected in the law.* Himself a distinguished judge, Posner does not follow his own prescription, as, of course, he cannot, without disregarding the distinction between legislation and adjudication.† So long as he allows that a rule may have force as a rule – not because it is right but because it is the rule – he has to accept the place of analogical reasoning to mediate between the rule and the facts, although he rightly inveighs against its casual or careless use. The resources that he commends are so valuable, as he says, not because they enable a judge to dispense with analogical reasoning but because they help to ensure that the analogy is sound.

In a recent book, Posner has indicated that he does not fully accept that a rule of law has force as a rule. Rather, he approves a theory of adjudication that he calls "everyday pragmatism," "the method of inquiry used by ordinary people," who "[use] common sense to resolve problems."[14] Posner's

---

* Posner's influential theory of the economic foundations of law confronts this issue ambiguously. It is often unclear whether his theory is intended as analysis of the law as it is, which uncovers policies latent in it, or as a prescription for the law as it ought to be. See Richard A. Posner, *Economic Analysis of Law* (6th ed. 2003). If it is the former, the theory describes the work of judges; if the latter, it prescribes in the first instance for legislators and only interstitially (insofar as it also reveals policies latent in the law) for judges.

† For a lucid statement of the bounds within which a judge works, see Posner's opinion *in Scheiber v. Dolby Laboratories, Inc.*, 293 F.3d 1014 (7th Cir. 2002).

description of everyday pragmatism is dense and detailed, but its main points seem clear.[15] At the center is an empirical inquiry into the consequences of a decision one way or the other. The consequences that have to be considered are not only the direct and immediate consequences for the parties and others. Long-term, systemic consequences have also to be considered, including the consequences of the mode of adjudication itself. Posner approves, therefore, "the rule of law," understood to signify "a due regard (not exclusive, not precluding tradeoffs) for the political and social value of continuity, coherence, generality, impartiality, and predictability in the definition and administration of legal rights and duties."[16] Often, perhaps usually, the value of adhering to the law as it is (or, Posner would probably say, as it has been) will outweigh any bad consequences. Nevertheless, it is consequences that count, and if, "all things considered," the best consequences will follow from disregarding the law, the pragmatist judge should disregard it.[17] Adherence to the law because it is the law and for no other reason is not part of his duty or his creed.

The position that Posner takes is so contrary to the usual understanding that one wonders if he can really mean it.* And, indeed, one may believe that it is more a posture than a solid

---

* One might add in passing that in ordinary circumstances, "the method of inquiry of ordinary people" is far more likely to be the reasoning by analogy that he deplores than the full-blown empirical inquiry that he recommends.

position and means less than it pretends. For calculation of the short- and long-term consequences of adhering to the rule of law and the negative consequences of departing from it affords little scope for the empirical inquiries that Posner most prizes, so that the result of the calculation is bound to be impressionistic and indefinite. One may suppose, therefore, that it would be a very rare case in which a pragmatic judge's decision would differ significantly from that of his more traditional colleague. Furthermore, the latter judge's need to employ analogical reasoning to bring the law to ground in a concrete case affords some room within the traditional mode of adjudication for consideration of consequences. The more weighty the consequences urging the pragmatist to disregard some rule of law, the more likely they are to point away from the conclusion that it is, indeed, that rule of law that is applicable.

One might conclude, therefore, that everyday pragmatism is more a theory and an attitude than a practice with practical significance. But to posture in that way in support of an abstract theory is what Posner likes least.[18] He denies that pragmatism is reserved for exceptional cases "in which truly exigent circumstances . . . exert unbearable pressure,"[19] and he associates pragmatism with a political theory that undermines the distinction between adjudication and legislation that makes the rule of law so central to the former.[20] One can say only that the theory and practice that Posner espouses is a radical departure from both the jurisprudential and the common sense understanding of what adjudication is.

Brewer's more elaborate three-step procedure, which he offers as a defense of analogical reasoning in the law, is, in truth, not a response to the arguments that have been made against it, but an evasion of them. The analogy itself, having only an epistemic role as the inspiration for a hypothesized rule, has no bearing on the decision of a case or how it is justified. That, he says, depends on the same instrumental analysis that Posner endorses, as well as the test of consistency with other law.* The final, deductive step, which is no more than the formal application of a rule to facts for which it was expressly designed, conforms to the phantasm school's characterization of analogical argument as deductive reasoning. Brewer relies on this latter step to sustain the rule of law, which he values highly. But since the prior instrumental inquiry is itself unconstrained by the rule of law, the rule that is finally applied is likewise unconstrained. Insofar as he includes consistency with other rules of law among the tests to be applied in arriving at a rule, the rule of law is preserved, but only by

---

* Brewer, who is more concerned than Posner about law as a *system* of rules, emphasizes consistency with other rules more than Posner does. Taken fully at his word, Posner seems to regard consistency as relevant only insofar as it serves efficiency "all things considered."

means of the kind of analogical argument that he had thought to avoid.

There remains the objection that cast adrift from formal logic and empirical inquiry, analogical reasoning is unprincipled and incapable of sustaining a substantial conclusion. That objection is answered in the next chapter.

CHAPTER FOUR

Analogical Reasoning, Legal Education, and the Law

a. Analogical reasoning

How then do we do it? If an analogy is neither a suppressed deductive argument nor, certainly, an inductive argument, what is it, and why do we – ought we – have confidence in the conclusion? How do we account for perception of the complex similarities on which an analogical legal argument rests: the similarity between a steamboat and an inn, on which the court relied in *Adams*; between a "live" performance and the reception and transmission of a radio broadcast, as in *Jewell-LaSalle*; and between a telephone booth and a business office, a friend's apartment, and a taxicab, as in *Katz*? What guides the selection and reliance on one similarity among all the others that might be mentioned and a multitude of dissimilarities?

The theories dismissive of analogical reasoning that are discussed in previous chapters assume that the logic of deductive and inductive argument defines the bounds within which those questions must be answered; no answer being found there, they conclude that there is none and that an analogical argument, thus unconstrained, is too weak to support the weighty consequences of an adjudication. Answers are found, however, not in abstract reason but directly in our experience of the world.

The ability to reason analogically is a rich subject for investigation and analysis. Full discussion of the issues that it presents and of experimental results and explanatory theories is beyond the scope of this book. I go no further here than to indicate the lines of inquiry that confirm what we already know: that we rely on analogical reasoning, usually with considerable success, all the time, in life as in law. References for further study are included in a Note on Analogical Reasoning in Appendix A.

The evidence is convincing that the capacity for analogical reasoning is hard-wired in us (and, incidentally, in animals), and develops initially at a very early age – within the first twelve months.[1] It is not fundamentally distinct from the capacity, also hard-wired, to recognize the general in the particular – the redness of an apple, a fire engine, and a clown's nose – without which we should be unable to describe or to refer to anything that is not immediately present and which, therefore, is implicit in all learning. The idea of *relevant* similarity, which has been so much discussed in connection with analogical reasoning, emerges not much later, as soon as such recognition develops beyond the mere perception of similar stimuli – the color red – to include the capacity to sort one's perceptions into discrete entities that persist over time and remain the same even though some of their qualities change – a red apple, a red fire engine, a clown's red nose. The child puts down his apple and walks away. When he goes back to it later, someone has taken a bite out of it, and the child complains, because *his apple* is no longer just as it had been. When he sees a fire engine, he knows what it is because he has a toy fire engine, even though the toy is very much smaller than what he now looks at. The clown takes off his red nose, and the child claps (or cries), because the clown who now stands before him is the same clown, yet different. Interacting with a very young child from day to day, one can observe the child's puzzlement about such transformations gradually dissipate. For the present purpose, what is significant is that when the child identifies *his apple, a fire engine, the clown*, he not only perceives the similarity between what he saw before and what he sees now, but also, so far as the identification is concerned, looks past the differences between them, which may be very substantial and in another context would be critically important.

As the child's vocabulary and conceptual understanding expand, the ability to distinguish relevant and irrelevant similarity and difference increases in complexity, so that without hesitation he can, according to the context, refer to a toy as his toy, a fire truck, a truck, a gift from his uncle, a piggy bank, and so forth. Each of those references requires him to sort the characteristics of the same object, those that are relevant and those that are not, in a different way. If you ask him to show you another truck, another gift from Uncle Dan, or another piggy bank, he will sort other objects in ways that again require him to distinguish among relevant similarities and differences.

There are large psychological and epistemological questions about how this process is learned and applied and how it is to be understood, questions that may fairly be said to be about the nature of thought itself. There is no question, however, that the ability is acquired very early and that it cannot be assimilated or reduced to deductive reasoning.*

---

* "[S]urely there is nothing more basic to thought and language than our sense of similarity; our sorting of things into kinds. The usual general term, whether a common noun or a verb or an adjective, owes its generality to some resemblance among the things referred to. Indeed, learning to use a word depends on a double resemblance: first, a resemblance between the present circumstances and past circumstances in which the word was used, and second, a phonetic resemblance between the present utterance of the word and past utterances of it. And every reasonable expectation depends on resemblance of circumstances, together with our tendency to expect similar causes to have similar effects. . . . We cannot easily

For deductive reasoning depends on it. Unless one is able to identify an object as a member of a class despite its differences from other members of the class, no deductive inference is possible. Thus, according to Westen's account,* the child's description of his toy as a fire engine should be reconstructed in the following fashion: "Anything of whatever size that is red, has six wheels, carries a coiled hose and ladders... is a fire engine. This (toy) is red, has six wheels, carries a coiled hose and ladders.... Therefore, it is a fire engine." Aside from the pointlessness of such a reconstruction, which would bury ordinary speech under a deductive landslide, it does not do the work that Westen's account requires; the general proposition on which the deduction depends is itself dependent on the ability to identify relevant similarities composing a class of fire engines that includes,

imagine a more familiar or fundamental notion than this [notion of similarity], or a notion more ubiquitous in its applications.... And yet, strangely, there is something logically repugnant about it. For we are baffled when we try to relate the general notion of similarity significantly to logical terms." W. V. Quine, *Natural Kinds,* in W. V. Quine, *Ontological Relativity and Other Essays* 114, 116–117 (1969), reprinted in Hilary Kornblith, ed., *Naturalizing Epistemology* 57, 58–59 (2d ed. 1994).

"A standard of similarity is in some sense innate.... Moreover, [in behavioral terms]... it can be said equally of other animals that they have an innate standard of similarity too. It is part of our animal birthright. And, interestingly enough, it is characteristically animal in its lack of intellectual status. At any rate we noticed earlier how alien the notion is to mathematics and logic." Quine at 123, Kornblith at 63.

* See p. 110.

for some purposes and not others, both the real thing and the toy.*

There is, of course, a great difference between the perceptible similarities of things, like color and shape, and the more complex similarities that signal or explain their common behavior, on which analogies like those that served Edna and Charlie depend. One can see that an apple and a fire engine are the same color; but one cannot see that if he steps on an apple, it will be squashed and will not squeal (or sprout wings or...) or that if he pulls the lever on a toy fire truck, a siren will sound and the truck will not explode (or do a tap dance or...).† The latter requires awareness not only of how things appear to the senses but also of how they act on other things and react to the action of other things on them. This awareness begins later than the awareness of perceptual similarities like color and shape, at around the age of three.‡ Once the general

---

* I refer here to similarities among *things*: apples, fire engines, a clown's nose, and the like. There are also, of course, similarities and dissimilarities among actions or occurrences – swimming is more (less?) like running than walking; a storm is more (less?) like a fire than a flood – and among qualities – red is more like orange than blue; a trumpet sounds more like a tuba than a violin. How similarity and dissimilarity among discrete particulars are to be analyzed and explained is at the heart of the problem of universals, as it is called. For references, see the Note on Analogical Reasoning in Appendix A.

† The *locus classicus* is David Hume: "When I cast my eye on the *known qualities* of objects, I immediately discover that the relation of cause and effect depends not in the least on *them*." David Hume, *A Treatise of Human Nature* 77 (L.A. Selby-Bigge, ed., 1888).

‡ A common signal of a child's developing awareness of causal relations, all too familiar to the child's parents, is an unceasing flood of "Why?" questions. As the

notion of cause and effect has been acquired, however, such information – what qualities of things are associated in what circumstances with what effects – accumulates rapidly. Thereafter, it is as available to us as perceptual similarities and is itself commonly a basis on which we sort things into kinds. To refer to something as a "knife" requires one to understand that if something with a sharp edge is rubbed against something else – not all things, tomatoes but not rocks – the latter "breaks." Having that understanding, one can identify a thing as a knife and also understand an analogy between a knife and another kind of thing – an axe or a bolt of lightning – that has a similar effect. Some of the information that accumulates, that which is closest to our interests and activities, is gradually organized into a coherent whole that includes structural explanatory relationships. Much of it, like what Edna knows about wine stains and Charlie about car engines, much or most of the time simply accumulates as the lessons of experience, which are integrated imperfectly with other information, as the occasion demands. Even in this disordered state,

concept of causation falls into place and the differences among causes, reasons, and purposes are learned, the use of "Why?" questions becomes more discriminating, and some that were previously asked are dropped.

Whether there is a fundamental epistemological difference between awareness of simple perceptual similarities and awareness of causal regularities seems to me an open question, although I suspect that there is not. Both seem clearly to be learned, or perhaps one should say "acquired," from experience, and, certainly, neither can be taught as abstractions, not, at least, until it has been acquired from concrete instances.

it is variously available, and it is indispensable to navigating the course of our lives.

Until quite recently, the prevailing theory about the development of analogical reasoning in children was that the capacity arises in early adolescence.[3] Children younger than eleven or twelve were thought generally to be able to understand simple relationships (kitten/cat, puppy/dog) but not the "higher-order" structural relationship between two simple relationships (kitten : cat :: puppy : dog) that is the basis for an analogy.[4] Tests of children at various ages appeared to confirm this theory, which corresponded to a general account of child development that described stages of cognitive ability.[5] More recent work indicates that children reason analogically much earlier than had been thought, and it supports a different explanation for a child's inability to grasp an analogy: what the child lacks is not the capacity to reason analogically as such but the knowledge on which the analogy depends.[6] Until a child has learned that a kitten is a young cat and a puppy is a young dog, she will not understand an analogy that depends on the fact that a kitten and a puppy are younger versions of a cat and a dog. She is likely to understand an analogy that compares her to a kitten before she understands why her father calls her "Tadpole," although the relevant similarity in both cases is the same. Furthermore, coherent knowledge structures, in which pieces of information are embedded in a conceptual system and related integrally, serve analogical reasoning better than isolated fragments of discrete information.[7] A child is better able to identify the relevant similarity that associates a kitten, a puppy, a tadpole, and a caterpillar analogically if she has a general understanding about the development of living things. According to this "knowledge-based" account, for which the evidence is strong, analogical reasoning does not implicate a cognitive faculty distinct from ordinary processes of thought. Not cognitive ability as such but experience and the knowledge that goes with it are the keys to effective analogical reasoning. Once the necessary experience is absorbed and understood, the ability to use it analogically follows, as an incident of that same understanding.

The normatively freighted concepts that inform the law – responsibility, trust, fraud, and the like – are a step further away from perceptual similarities than explanatory concepts of cause and effect. There is, however, nothing to suggest that the capacity for analogical reasoning is different or operates differently in that context. Until a child has some conceptual understanding of what a moral imperative is, he will not be much impressed if he is asked, "How would you like it if someone did that to you?" Asking such a question of a small child, a parent may be baffled and frustrated by the response, "I won't let anyone do that to me." Once a child's understanding expands to include normative relations, their use analogically is not far behind, as the familiar exchange, "You shouldn't hit your sister" / "She hit me first," amply shows.

The experimental findings in cognitive and developmental psychology as well as patterns of ordinary thought that we all recognize give no support to accounts of analogical reasoning according to which the critical notion of relevant similarity is unexplained or mysterious or is attributed to an obscure and ineffable "intuition." Relevance has the same meaning in this context that it has in others. Without having any general rule or principle to work with, we often can tell with reasonable assurance what is likely to be relevant, because we have had more or less similar experiences in the past and are able to call them to mind and because we have a general sense, also acquired from experience, of how things work, what accounted for the past experience and is likely, in similar circumstances, to have the same effect.* Sometimes experience fails us. Who would have thought that the mold that forms on bread and other foods would be the source of an invaluable medicine?[8] But over a large range, our experience is orderly and serves

---

* To say that we are able to draw an analogy between source and target without knowing a general rule or principle that accounts for it is not, of course, to say that there is no such principle. The predictability of experience depends on the stability of causal relationships; it is the task of science to capture and express that stability in explanatory principles.

us well. If it were not, if stepping on an apple were as likely to make it cry out or sprout wings as to squash it, and so forth, we should have more to concern us than how to make a good analogy.

The same basis of understanding applies in law. No rule declares generally that inns and steamboats, or operators of inns and operators of steamboats, are alike – for many purposes they are not – or that all situations in which one person trusts another and the latter is subject to temptation should be treated alike – for many purposes they should not. Nevertheless, someone who is familiar with the law of torts would readily suppose that the rule about an innkeeper's liability has a bearing on a question about the liability of a steamboat operator, not because he has in mind a rule that applies to both but because his knowledge of the law tells him that the similarities between them relate to factors that commonly have a bearing on liability. So also, if his knowledge extends so far, it would occur to him that there is another rule, about the operator of a railroad sleeping car, which also may be relevant and points in a different direction. More general knowledge about the law of torts and still more general understanding of the law's approach to matters of commercial dealing and personal and interpersonal responsibility may suggest other relevant rules and will help him to assess the comparative relevance of one rule or another. (It is in this manner that the "vertical and horizontal ordering" of justificatory principles, about which Ronald Dworkin has written, takes hold.*) In the same way, he will quickly dismiss most of the concrete details of the situation before him, like the menu for dinner and what Adams wore to bed, as irrelevant to the defendant's liability, not because he knows and can recite a multitude of rules so providing but because his accumulated experience in the law tells him that those facts are not likely to count.

After the decision in *Olmstead* in 1928, it would have been obvious to someone with knowledge of that case that an invasion of privacy that did not involve a physical trespass probably did not violate the Fourth Amendment, even though the precise circumstances were quite different. There was no all-embracing rule to that effect, however, and he would have had to rely on his more general knowledge of the Fourth Amendment and, more broadly, rules about trespass in the law of property to be sure that some nontrespassory intrusion other than eavesdropping was likewise not a violation. Forty years later, when *Katz* was decided, there was not a rule that made the absence of a trespass irrelevant. But someone who had followed the progression of cases since *Olmstead* would have been aware that the requirement of a trespass was

* See p. 7.

under attack, and a more general awareness of the recent extension of a defendant's constitutional rights in other respects might well have suggested that the element of a trespass was no longer as relevant as a person's reasonable expectation of privacy in the circumstances. For that reason, the government's brief in *Katz* argued that there could be no violation of the Fourth Amendment in the absence of a trespass, but, plainly aware that the rule of *Olmstead* was vulnerable, it argued on other grounds that eavesdropping on Katz's telephone conversation did not violate his rights under the Fourth Amendment, even if the requirement of a trespass were eliminated.*

Although the need to reason analogically is common to all legal systems that subscribe to the rule of law, one would not expect the analogies that are used to be everywhere the same, even when the legal issues addressed are alike. The reasoning, including analogical reasoning, of a British court is likely to be more comprehensible to an American lawyer than the reasoning of a French court, because of the common British and American legal heritage, although the divergence of the two, as well as all the differences between British and American life generally, would potentially interfere. Such comparisons aside, our ability to get along in the law depends on its

* See p. 57n.

reasonable predictability. In this respect, the coherence and stability of a legal order is an analogue of the orderliness of nature. The analogy is not complete, because our knowledge of the natural order depends on the overriding premise that its regularities are part of an objective reality that is there to be discovered. Regularities of the legal order, on the other hand, are the product of human design and have to be constructed. Nevertheless, in an ongoing legal order, they enable us to subject analogies in the law to the ordinary demands of substantive reasonableness, in light of what we know.

In short, support for the analogy on which an analogical legal argument depends is found in its legal context or, more simply, in the law itself. Those who insist that there is no basis for validating a legal argument except by deduction or induction suppose that lawyers and judges make their arguments in a vacuum, as if they have no more reason to choose one analogy over another than the visitor from Mars who is asked to explain why the lawn is wet.* But that is as false in law as it is in ordinary affairs. If Edna, relying on the fact that salt and talcum powder are both white, had suggested to Mary that she add a dash of talcum powder to the soup, Mary would have had good reason to prefer her usual recipe, even though she

* See p. 23.

probably knows nothing about the properties of sodium chloride – salt – or hydrous magnesium silicate – talc. As Hume observed, so far as one can tell from appearances, talcum powder is as likely to improve the taste of soup as salt. A child, making make-believe soup, might well stir in some talcum powder. But Mary knows better; her accumulated knowledge and experience tell her that talcum powder belongs in the medicine cabinet and not the spice rack. Some analogies *are* better than others, not just because they happen to appeal to one's imagination or individual sensibility but because they correspond more closely to our experience and understanding.

So also in the law. If Adams's lawyer had argued that the steamboat operator was liable for Adams's loss because the steamboat provided musical entertainment after dinner, as do many inns, or if the steamboat operator's lawyer had argued that it was not liable because Adams had slept in the nude, the judge might reasonably have been perplexed, because nothing in the law of torts or elsewhere in the law supported the suggestion that a shipboard concert or a person's nocturnal (un)dress has anything to do with liability for a loss by theft. On the other hand, the relation between the parties, more particularly the confidence of a guest or passenger in an innkeeper's or steamboat operator's honesty, and the latters' temptation to betray that confidence are just the sort of consideration that tort law and the more general legal background indicated were relevant.

The legal knowledge and experience that lawyers and judges bring to the facts of a case tell them, just as Mary's knowledge and experience tell her, that some similarities count for the matter at hand and others do not. Their ability to make such distinctions is no more mysterious in the one case than in the other. If a legal analogy cannot be put to the test in the same way that a practical analogy can, it is nevertheless subject to tests of consistency and coherence with rules of law that together indicate the relevance of particular facts to the issue in question, although neither individually nor collectively do they prescribe conclusively for the specific situation.* If rules that are directly relevant are silent or inadequate to settle the matter, then there is resort to other, more remote rules, for whatever light they may shed. In a close case, there may finally be a choice between two alternatives – inns or railroad sleeping cars – that no rule alone or in combination with others resolves completely. The disagreement that remains after a case has been fully argued and considered is not unique to the law, nor is it a defect. It is the inevitable concomitant of the effort to confine the variety of human experience within general rules.

---

* It is these tests of consistency and coherence that lend color to the claim that analogical reasoning is really deductive.

b. The case method

Christopher Columbus Langdell, recently appointed Professor and Dean of the Harvard Law School,* introduced the case method of legal education in his first class on Contracts in 1870.[9] He had two objectives. The first was to establish law as a science, by applying a scientific method of analysis to reported cases, which he regarded as raw material comparable to experimental data in the physical sciences. The second was to reform legal education. Pedagogy too would employ the method of science; as if in a laboratory, students would extract legal doctrines from the cases themselves, instead of receiving them in lectures and treatises. Langdell's jurisprudential ambition to place law on a scientific footing was not successful (although he himself never abandoned it).[10] It became a subject of derision, lampooned as "mechanical jurisprudence," and was a chief target of the Legal Realists in the early

---

* Charles William Eliot, who had become president of Harvard University in 1869, appointed Langdell the Dane Professor of Law on January 6, 1870. 2 Charles Warren, *History of the Harvard Law School and of Early Legal Conditions in America* 354, 359 (1908). Langdell gave his first lectures, on Negotiable Paper and Partnership, in the spring term. Id. at 363. On September 27, 1870, the Faculty of Law held its first formal meeting, and it elected Langdell as the Law School's first dean, id. at 370–371, evidently because no one else on the faculty was interested in the job. Charles W. Eliot, *Langdell and the Law School*, 33 Harv. L. Rev. 518, 519 (1920). See William P. LaPiana, *Logic and Experience*, 11–14 (1994). Eliot became a committed supporter of the case method and had much to do with its establishment at Harvard and elsewhere. Anthony Chase, *The Birth of the Modern Law School*, 23 Am. J. Legal Hist. 329 (1979).

twentieth century.[11] It has now no significant support. The triumph of Langdell's pedagogy, on the other hand, is complete. In part because of its adoption and championing of the "case method" of instruction, Harvard Law School became under Langdell's deanship the leading law school in the country.[12] More than a hundred years later, the case method remains the standard form of legal instruction. Although the texts that students read now contain much more than cases (mostly appellate opinions), which were the sole material of Langdell's courses, they are still known as "casebooks," and cases still dominate their content. Oddly, the reasons for the failure of Langdell's first objective and for the success of the second are closely related.

The idea that law could be studied scientifically did not originate with Langdell; the reference to science did not necessarily mean more than that, one way or another, law is a body of knowledge, composed of true principles that can be studied and learned. Legal doctrine, it was supposed, composes a coherent, logically orderly system, which provides a correct outcome for every case. According to a view prominent in the first half of the nineteenth century, at the apex of the system are transcendental principles of natural justice and reason, from which the doctrine is deduced. Therefore, although decisions in actual cases are evidence of the law, they are not to be relied on entirely, because judges err and cases may be in conflict. The effort of the legal scientist is to discern the true first principles and to work from there.* Langdell's notion of legal science was quite different. The doctrines of the law, he argued, are not to be traced to transcendental principles, but are to be found exclusively in cases. The study of cases themselves, scientifically pursued, would, he thought, yield a small number of fundamental principles from which the outcomes of concrete cases follow.[13] How, without circularity, the outcome in particular cases could be deduced from the hierarchy of principles and at the same time provide the raw material from which the principles are derived inductively remained obscure.[14]

There are a number of reasons to reject so doctrinaire (if not, indeed, mechanical) a view of the judicial function, not least its tendency to treat the prescriptive content of the law and the descriptive statements of science as equivalent. As a strictly formal matter, aside from the circularity of regarding the law as both an inductive science and as a deductive, hermetically sealed system, what Langdell's conception of the law

---

* Id. at 29–38. So, for example, Nathan Dane observed in the Introduction to his Abridgment, a highly regarded digest of American law and standard work: "Having treated a subject, or an important case, in its parts, it has been found useful, if not necessary, to make, in some cases, some remarks, comments, or notes, to explain, not only for the benefit of those who most need explanation, but to caution against admitting judicial decisions as authorities, where the remote principle, on which they were made, is not admitted." 1 Nathan Dane, *A General Abridgment and Digest of American Law* vii (1823).

omitted was a means for bridging the gap between facts and law, or law and facts. It included no method of reasoning from the bottom up, from the decision of a case to a rule broader than the facts of the case itself, nor a method of reasoning from the top down, from a rule to facts to which the rule does not in terms apply. Nor was there anything in legal science as Langdell conceived it that corresponds to the experimental results by which the descriptive regularities of natural science are corrected and confirmed. It was into this gap that the Legal Realists and, more recently, adherents of Critical Legal Studies poured their scornful demonstrations that a rule of law isolated from its context could be made to yield precisely contrary conclusions.[15]

In class, however, under the direction of someone who is knowledgeable about the law, the case method proved to be an excellent pedagogical technique to exercise students' capacity for analogical reasoning at the same time that they acquire the knowledge of the law that informs the capacity. The full-scale classroom discussion of a case typically begins, as Langdell began his class on Contracts in 1870,[16] with a request that a student "state the facts." The reason for that is not simply to mirror the usual structure of a lawyer's argument or the opinion of a court. Rather, it is because what is to be gleaned from the opinion first of all is the law as it applies specifically to the facts of that case. Thereafter, the sequence of questions varies according to professorial style, but the course of discussion typically follows a common pattern. Students are asked what arguments for each side the court considered in its opinion and how it disposed of them, whether there are other persuasive arguments that the court did not consider, what the outcome of the case and the holding – the rule of law that determined the outcome – are, and, finally, whether the court's reasoning and its result are sound. Discussing the arguments and the outcome, students are expected to relate the facts of the case to relevant rules of law that they have encountered in other cases and to consider whether the outcome is consistent with those rules.* So also, the holding will be tested by comparing it with the holdings of other cases that are more or less similar. Just what the holding is may itself be a topic for discussion; at its narrowest, the holding will apply only to the very facts of the case, and stated more broadly, it will apply to other situations in which the facts may be considerably different. Throughout this discussion, students' understanding of the law is likely to be tested by questions requiring them to apply the putative holding and related rules to a series of "hypos," hypothetical situations in which the facts vary from the actual facts, which progress from a small variation to larger

---

* This description applies most fully to "common law" subjects that typically are part of the first-year curriculum, like torts, contracts, and property. In courses that depend heavily on statutory material, the relevant rules will be derived from a statute (as interpreted in prior cases).

and larger ones or from a very large variation to smaller and smaller ones and finally to one that is scarcely distinguishable from the actual facts. (Hence the so-called slippery slope on which a student engaged in such a discussion is likely to find himself standing.) Thus, the discussion is always brought back to the question whether the holding of the case applies to particular facts, which is pursued dialectically by the variation of one fact or another and the increasingly precise enunciation of the holding itself.* The class discussion thus mirrors the work of lawyers and judges in the course of adjudication. It is a continuous exercise in analogical reasoning (as well as, of course, much else), a correct statement of the law being pursued by the progressive inclusion of variant facts within, or their exclusion from, its range of application.

Early in their legal education, it occurs to many students that this method of instruction is uncommonly wasteful: If the professor knows the law, why doesn't she tell the students what it is and let them learn it, instead of beating around the bush

---

* To the dismay of some students in their first weeks at law school (and sometimes later), there may be small place in the discussion for consideration of how the decision in the case affected the parties, whether it was fair, or whether it would serve the public interest if it were applied generally. For the teacher may temporarily (or occasionally, if the teacher is of a certain bent, permanently) foreclose such questions by insisting that the question before the class is what the law *is* and not what the law *ought* to be. In my own view, although it is often important to make the distinction between the two questions, the latter question is as important as the former. Not only is the moral evaluation of law important in itself, but also, because such evaluation is part of the context that determines the relevance of one analogy or another, it has a bearing on what the law is.

and, very likely, finally leaving them in the dark anyway? Not infrequently, after the first few weeks students find themselves bewildered. If they express their bewilderment to the professor, she is likely to reply, "Don't worry. It will come together." And, usually, by the end of the semester, it does. Learning the law means more than memorizing the rules that have been set down in past cases, even a very large number of them; it means understanding how the rules would be applied to other cases with different facts. Although Langdell himself did not see it just that way, the genius of the case method is that it equips students to understand legal doctrine in use, not only the "black letter rule" but also what specific details in a novel situation may have a bearing on whether and how the rule is applied. Time spent studying the *Adams* case has value beyond the rule that a steamboat operator, in those particular circumstances, is liable as an insurer for a passenger's loss. A student who appreciates the reasoning as well as the result will take away also a more general sense of the kind of consideration that affects one person's liability for another's loss, which, together with the lessons of other more or less similar cases, may apply not only in a subsequent case having to do with the liability of a steamboat operator in somewhat different circumstances but also in a case involving the liability of an airplane carrier or a taxicab driver or, even more remotely, the case of someone who gives bad advice about how to remove a stain from a tablecloth. The facts of all of those cases will afford some basis for arguing that the rule or the reasoning in *Adams* should be applied, as well as a basis for arguing that it should not. The discussion in class, as later in practice, proceeds by analogical reasoning. That is what "thinking like a lawyer" means.

c. The rule of law

The large, unexceptional role that analogical reasoning plays in the affairs of everyday life invites attention to the resistance on theoretical grounds to acknowledging its role in the law, all the more so because argument "by analogy" is widely recognized as a distinctive characteristic of legal reasoning. The persistent effort of legal scholars to downgrade analogical reasoning (except, perhaps, as a useful ploy), if not, indeed, to dismiss it altogether, is simply ignored by the lawyers and judges who regularly employ it. On the face of the matter, the lawyers and judges have the better of it. Why ought our inability to demonstrate the validity of an analogical argument as if it were a logical proof or to verify it experimentally be regarded as an obstacle in law any more than it is in ordinary affairs? Scholars and law students, no less than lawyers and judges, debate the merits of legal arguments and usually reach a measure of agreement. In view of the range and variety of the issues and the consequences for the parties, it is hardly surprising that there are close cases and disagreement about the outcomes. If certainty is not attainable, nevertheless a reasonable certitude generally is. There are widely shared criteria for appraising an argument that depends significantly on the use of analogy, and it is evident that the ability to make such arguments effectively has much to do with professional competence in the law.

No single idea contributes more to the respect that Americans have for their government and legal system than that they are subject to the rule of law: Ours is a "government of laws, and not of men."* Just what the rule of law signifies is a good deal more complex than John Marshall's familiar aphorism suggests.[17] Common to all its more particular meanings, however, is the understanding that the law is available to be known in advance by those who are entrusted with its application. It is closely connected to the requirements of accessibility

---

* *Marbury v. Madison*, 5 U.S. (1 Cranch.) 137, 163 (1803). John Adams had used the phrase earlier in a draft of a constitution for Massachusetts. See Massachusetts Constitution of 1780, pt. 1, art. xxx, in Charles Kettleborough, ed., *The State Constitutions* 658 (1918). See id at 654n. James Harrington had used the phrase more than a hundred years before that in *The Commonwealth of Oceana* (1656). See *The Political Works of James Harrington* 155, 182 (J.G.A. Pocock, ed., 1977). By referring only to Americans, I do not mean to express doubt that the rule of law is a universal, or well-nigh universal, ideal. There are, of course, and have been, actual societies in which the rule of law as it is commonly understood does not prevail.

and clarity, which enable persons who are willing to do so to conform their conduct to the law.[18] It speaks most directly, however, not to those who comply but to those who declare the law. They are not to decide for themselves what the law is but are to seek it out, to discover and apply it as it is.*

It is easy to grasp why analogical arguments may appear to subvert the rule of law. If the question is isolated from its legal context, who can say with any assurance whether a steamboat is more like an inn or a railroad sleeping car, or even specify how the question is to be answered? Yet, if the answer is indeterminate in any particular case until the question has been answered *in that case*, must not a decision that rests on the answer likewise be indeterminate? And must not the law of that case – the rights and obligations of the parties – then be a function of the subjective judgment of whoever it is who determines the analogy? Nor does the decision once made avoid a like indeterminacy in the future. Subsequent cases that present different facts may be determined to call for application of a different analogy. Is not law so grounded a rule of men, by any other name, and not a rule of law at all?†

---

* Even that apparently simple statement is freighted with complexities. In a sense, to ask what the law *is* rather than what it *ought to be* commits one to the rule of law; but such verbal maneuvers do not address the underlying issues.

† Doubts of this kind do not infect only cases applying rules derived from judicial opinions. They may arise whenever a court is called on to apply a rule to facts not precisely like any to which it has previously been applied. Even if the rule is contained in an authoritative text, like a statute or an express judicial

It is no great matter if Mary's tablecloth does not come clean or Charlie's lawn mower won't start. One can always try something else. In law, not only may getting it wrong have large, often unpredictable consequences for the losing party, but also one of the most important normative dimensions of our experience is compromised. Law claims our allegiance and, having a monopoly of legitimate force, demands our compliance. The effort to bolster the rational sufficiency of analogical legal argument is prompted by concern that if the adjudicative process is insufficient rationally, it is insufficient normatively as well. Any lingering uncertainty about the outcome of a case is thought to reflect uncertainty about what the law is and to that extent to reveal a breach in the law itself. If the same uncertainty attaches to any analogical argument, nevertheless, the implications outside the law are not so far-reaching.

Without quite saying so, those who reject analogical legal reasoning make the same demand of law that drove the discredited quest for a "legal science" in the nineteenth century. From that perspective, however useful an analogy may be to persuade, being neither an inductive nor a deductive argument, it has no credentials in reason, so that to rest a decision to any extent on an analogical argument

precedent, the authority of the text is not dispositive of its own interpretation. See pp. 88–91.

[149]

undermines its authority. Brewer makes that point explicitly. Rejecting both the "skeptical" and the "mystical" accounts of analogy,* he says that his primary aim is to show that an analogical argument is far more disciplined intellectually and has "a much higher degree of *rational force*" than is generally allowed.[19] He accomplishes his aim by embedding an analogy in a sequence of inductive and deductive reasoning, in which it has only an incidental role and no role at all in justifying the conclusion. A similar concern is evident in Posner's observations that lawyers' training and experience equip them with "essentially casuistic tools" and that "legal reasoning is, essentially, debaters' reasoning," which he contrasts unfavorably with empirically grounded inductive reasoning.[20] So also, the phantasm school reconstructs an analogical argument as a deductive inference.

A requirement that law be demonstrable (or verifiable) and certain is no less misconceived as a standard by which to measure the rule of law than it is as a program by which to achieve it. Rationality does not demand so much. The effort to proceed by rule dictates only that rules, including their range of application, be stated as clearly as the subject matter permits and that the persons who are charged to apply the rules try conscientiously to abide by their terms and have the necessary

---

* See pp. 30–32.

experience and learning to do so. It calls for official integrity, not the elimination of human judgment. The requirement of determinateness, after all, is a requirement that the rules have bounds that are reasonable and practically accessible, not a requirement that the bounds be self-executing.

There is no guarantee that a rule of law will be applied correctly. The intervention of human judgment makes it possible that a decision will be mistaken, or foolish, or biased, or perverse. Room for human judgment is room for all the errors of which human beings are capable. As Justice Jackson famously observed of the Supreme Court, "We are not final because we are infallible, but we are infallible only because we are final."[21] Recognizing the possibility of error, one can adopt practices that reduce its likelihood: providing ample opportunity for debate and discussion, avoiding obscure language that conveys no clear meaning, explaining decisions fully and exposing the explanation to official review or simply the informed consideration of others. Failure in any of these respects may, indeed, compromise the rule of law. Sometimes, despite the best effort, the application of a rule will be contested, and it will not be possible to say confidently what the right answer is.* In the

---

* Ronald Dworkin has made much in his jurisprudence of the thesis that an adjudicated case has a "right answer." See Ronald Dworkin, *Hard Cases*, 88 Harv. L. Rev. 1057 (1975), reprinted in Ronald Dworkin, *Taking Rights Seriously* 81–130 (1977); Ronald Dworkin, *No Right Answer?*, 53 N.Y.U. L. Rev. 1 (1978), reprinted in Ronald Dworkin, *A Matter of Principle* 119–145 (1985). He is clear, however,

largest sense, recognition of that uncertainty does not mark a departure from the rule of law. On the contrary, it confirms it.

The impulse to insulate law from the fallibility of human judgment has a long history. It springs from the conviction that the very notion of law, and with it justice, lacks meaning unless it is unequivocal; not merely reasonable but, in some sense, true. How can a rule or a decision be law, it is thought, if its credentials are only the reasonableness and good faith of the persons who declare it? If the law's claim to the authority of

that there is no procedure for demonstrating what the right answer is and that reasonable lawyers and judges may and often do disagree about what the right answer is. *Taking Rights Seriously,* above, at 81. His thesis is, in the first instance, a forceful defense of the sufficiency of law and, therefore, a defense of the rule of law, which builds on his model of law as a coherent, comprehensive body of rules. See p. 7. In the context of adjudication, he argues, the law contains within itself the ultimate political and moral principles on which law finally depends. See *Taking Rights Seriously,* at 105. Accordingly, a judge making the "justificatory ascent" from a legal rule must, even at the highest level, not look to sources outside the law but must search out the principles embodied within it. At that level of justification, his thesis may be thought to prescribe an attitude more than a method; whichever it is, adherence to the rule of law is its core. Abstracted from the concrete task of adjudication and considered as a theory about the nature of law, Dworkin's right-answer thesis lends itself to the claim that the positive law, properly conceived, generates the criteria of its own validity. In his fully developed theory, which he calls "law as integrity," Dworkin seems to take that position, which he grounds not on the substance of the laws but on the nature of law as such. He acknowledges that this view of law incorporates substantive normative principles, but they are, he asserts, implications of the notion of law as the source of order in a human community. See generally Ronald Dworkin, *Law's Empire* 87–275 (1986). In this aspect, the theory has an affinity with theories of natural law, see pp. 154–160, an affinity that Dworkin acknowledges. See *Law's Empire* at 35–36, 263, 297; Ronald Dworkin, *"Natural" Law Revisited,* 34 U. Fla. L. Rev. 165 (1982). For a critical assessment of the theory, see Lloyd L. Weinreb, *Natural Law and Justice* 117–122 (1987).

reason rests on so infirm a foundation, must one not conclude that, after all is said, its authority is not that of reason but only the will of those who have the power to enforce it?

The question can be traced in Western thought to the debate in classical Athens between those, like Plato, who believed that the cosmos is normatively ordered, which order is timeless and true, and those, notably the Sophists, who believed that the normative order of human existence is a matter of convention only, established by the effort of human beings themselves.* For the former, laws of a human community that contravene the normative order of the cosmos – the normative natural order – are not true law and in the course of time are falsified; ultimately, each person has his due, whatever the community's own laws might provide to the contrary. For the latter, the concepts of right and wrong, justice and desert, have meaning only as human constructs, which have no source of validity beyond the community's own established normative order. Later, under the influence of Christian theology, the Platonic view embraced the idea of a divine Creator,

---

* In Protagoras's phrase, "man is the measure of all things." Quoted in Plato, *Theaetetus*160d (F.M. Cornford, trans.), in Edith Hamilton and Huntington Cairns, eds., *The Collected Dialogues of Plato* 866 (1961). To say that norms are conventional did not imply that they are insignificant ("merely conventional," as we might say) or easily changed. The Greek word *nomos*, translated here as "convention," might refer to laws of great importance and long standing; it took its meaning in large part from its opposition to *physis*, the term used to describe the natural order. For a brief introduction and references, see Weinreb, p. 152n., at 26–30.

who provides alike for the natural order and for humankind, for whom God's Providence is law, accessible to reason and, therefore, enabling human beings to have a share in their own providence. It was a corollary of this view that human laws that do not conform to the providential order are not true law. The opposed view insisted that even as a matter of God's Providence, the natural order and the law for humankind are products of will, God's will, which is not subordinate to reason and, therefore, not accessible to human reason.* Human law might be contrary to God's will, but there are no certain means to determine whether that is so and, therefore, no certain test of the law's validity external to the law itself. Underlying the metaphysical complexities of these positions was a profound effort to situate the human experience of freedom and the notion of individual responsibility and desert within the causal order of nature.[22]

The jurisprudential debate has, for the most part, drawn back from its metaphysical origins. United within the camp of natural law are theories that maintain one way or another that it is intelligible to speak of laws as true or not true, that human reason can discern the true law, and that the obligatory

---

* So, it was debated whether God willed what was (objectively) good, or the good was whatever God willed, because God willed it. The theological terms of the debate masked the question that was at the bottom of it: whether the norms of human behavior are true or real and can be found out by human reason. See Weinreb, p. 152n., at 64–65.

character of law attaches fully only to true law.[23] Theories of legal positivism assert that law is entirely a product of human effort, that human reason can discern no objective truth against which law can be measured, and that the obligatory character of law generally or of particular laws cannot be demonstrated with certainty. The moral evaluation of law, which natural law regards as intrinsic to its nature, is regarded by legal positivism as no less important, but nevertheless as separate from the question of what the law is. The phenomenon of Nazism presented the issue starkly. Proponents of natural law asked: What moral claim to our allegiance can the idea of law have, if it can attach to unspeakable evil?* To which legal positivists replied: Even, or especially, in those extreme circumstances, we bear the burden of moral judgment, for which there is no responsibility except our own and from which there is no escape.†[24]

---

* So, Fuller argued that the dilemma that legal positivism poses between obeying a thoroughly evil statute, which has yet some claim to obedience, and doing what we think right and decent "has the verbal formulation of a problem, but the problem it states makes no sense. It is like saying I have to choose between giving food to a starving man and being mimsy with the borogoves." Lon L. Fuller, *Positivism and Fidelity to Law – A Reply to Professor Hart*, 71 Harv. L. Rev. 630, 656 (1958).

† "To use in the description of the interpretation of laws the suggested terminology of a fusion or inability to separate what is law and ought to be will serve . . . only to conceal the facts, that here if anywhere we live among uncertainties between which we have to choose, and that the existing law imposes only limits on our choice and not the choice itself." H.L.A. Hart, *Positivism and the Separation of Law and Morals*, 71 Harv. L. Rev. 593, 629 (1958).

As the Nazi experience has receded, the urgency of the search for objectivity in the law has lessened. The terms of the debate have changed, but the debate continues. Among recent scholars in contemporary American jurisprudence who have an affinity with the natural law tradition are those who believe that the answer to many, or most, constitutional questions can be determined with certainty, either because the "plain meaning" of the constitutional text leaves no room for disagreement or because the "original intent" of the Framers of the Constitution, revealed by the text and sometimes by supplementary materials, is certain and permits no deviation. It will perhaps seem contrary to the notion of natural law to associate it with the Constitution, which is itself the product of human effort and compromise. It may seem still further from the notion of natural law to associate with it those who trace constitutional law to the intent of the Framers, a particular group of human actors, with variable, often contentious ideas and motivations. Not infrequently, however, those who rely on "original intent" as the dispositive answer to current controversies treat the Constitution simply as an authoritative – objectively valid – text and use original intent as a formula to avoid the need for interpreting the text.

The affinity between "originalism," as it is called, and natural law is not based on their agreement about substantive issues. Originalism supports many rules as a matter of constitutional law that generally have no place in doctrines of natural law. Likewise, natural law is commonly thought to affirm certain human rights that an originalist does not recognize as constitutional rights, because he cannot locate them in the text of the Constitution, although, perhaps, he would support their statutory enactment. Their affinity is, rather, a common attitude toward questions about the law and a common approach to their resolution. Both regard certainty about what the law is not only as desirable but also as achievable and as a criterion of true law, not in every case, but in many and the most important. Originalists rely on the Constitution in much the way that adherents of natural law rely on human reason, by itself or with some metaphysical support. They are alike prone to dismiss disagreement with their conclusions as simply a mistake.

Successors to legal positivism include those who believe that the Constitution provides no certain answer even for constitutional questions. Although the text of the Constitution, interpreted in light of the intention of the Framers, so far as it is known, is the starting point for the decision of constitutional issues, it is not the end. The vast social, political, and economic changes between the eighteenth century and the present have also to be considered. Many issues that concern us now were simply not conceived in the same way when the Constitution was written. Application of the text and the original intent behind it to our current circumstances calls inescapably for fallible human judgment and, perforce, opens the way to uncertainty.

The connection between the jurisprudential debate and matters of constitutional interpretation is illustrated clearly, if a little perversely, by a debate in the 1940s and 1950s between Justice Black and Justice Frankfurter about the application to state criminal proceedings of specific provisions of the Bill of Rights, which, as drafted, applies only to the federal government. Justice Black argued that all the provisions having to do with criminal process had been incorporated into the Due Process Clause of the Fourteenth Amendment, which applies to the states, and that the provisions were thereby made applicable to the states.[25] Justice Frankfurter rejected such wholesale incorporation; instead, he argued that the Due Process Clause has an "independent potency," which absorbs some provisions of the Bill of Rights and not others, according to their content, as part of the meaning of due process.[26] Accordingly, not all the provisions of the Bill of Rights but only those that had been absorbed apply to the states.[27] Part of their disagreement had to do with the intention of the drafters of the Due Process Clause; Justice Black asserted and Justice Frankfurter denied that they had intended to incorporate the provisions of the Bill of Rights that were in question.[28]

Each side also deployed considerations of federal policy, Black urging that federalism did not, and Frankfurter that it did, justify having different criminal procedures in federal and state courts. But the heart of the matter lay deeper. Black's insistence on incorporating the text of the various provisions of the Bill of Rights, without any selectivity, was driven by belief that, at least at the constitutional level, law could, and should, satisfy objective criteria, which are proof against subjective individual judgment. His incorporation thesis, he believed, achieved that, because in his view the meaning of the incorporated provisions was known. He derided what he called Frankfurter's "natural law" approach, which, he said, left judges free to pick and choose which provisions to apply and how to apply them, according to their individual sense of justice.[29] Frankfurter acknowledged the burden of decision and the possibility of error, but he insisted that the traditions of the judiciary and the discipline and detachment of conscientious judges provided more guidance than the automatic application of supposed plain meanings of selected constitutional language, which, he said, would lead inevitably to arbitrary results.[30]

In fact, although Frankfurter did not disclaim the label of natural law, it was Black himself who took the characteristic natural law position. Placing overriding value on certainty, he thought that he achieved it by relying directly on the words of the Constitution, which had a definite meaning and provided an objective test for the correct result.* Frankfurter, accepting the burden of decision and the possibility of error, made room in his constitutional theory for the incertitudes of legal positivism.

The connection between the jurisprudential debate (and within it, the debate about constitutional meaning) and the debate about the place of analogical reasoning in adjudication is evident. There is, on one hand, a demand for certainty and a belief that it is achievable, despite the persistence of disagreements in fact and an inability to overcome them, except as a matter of personal conviction. On the other hand, there is acceptance of uncertainty and recognition that disagreement is not always to be avoided and may even be conducive to a satisfactory outcome. Set against the background of this larger debate, discussion of analogical reasoning takes

---

* Black's belief that incorporation of the clauses of the Bill of Rights would eliminate the need for judicial judgment was severely tested when the Court declared that the Sixth Amendment's provision for trial by jury, as incorporated and made applicable to the states, does not mean that a jury has to be composed of twelve persons, although it had previously been so interpreted as applied to federal trials. *Williams v. Florida*, 399 U.S. 78 (1970). Agreeing with that conclusion, Black said that it followed "solely as a necessary consequence of our duty to re-examine prior decisions to reach the correct constitutional meaning in each case." Id. at 107 (Black, J., concurring). Prior decisions to the contrary "were based...on an improper interpretation" of the Sixth Amendment. Id. He did not explain how the Court's duty could be performed without the exercise of human, that is to say, fallible judgment. Frankfurter, who was no longer on the Court when *Williams* was decided, would not have accepted the "correction." See *Rochin v. California*, 342 U.S. 165, 169–170 (1952).

on greater significance. Law gives expression to a community's values and in turn shapes the community and affects conduct in ways vastly more pervasive and far-reaching than the judgments of a court. Nevertheless, adjudication is the means by which law takes hold formally and finally and, in a sense, has its concrete being. If close attention to the process of adjudication provides no guarantee that the laws applied are sound, it is also true that until the laws are applied, they remain general and abstract and, however sound in principle, are vulnerable to distortion and error. It is, therefore, of first importance that the adjudicative process be understood.

Analogical reasoning is central to that process. It allows us to govern our lives according to general rules without disclaiming the singularity of human experience. The goal is not certainty but a reasonable assurance that rules are applied as predictably and evenhandedly as the variousness of human behavior permits. Nor can certainty be achieved by reconstituting analogical reasoning as, or supplanting it with, inductive or deductive arguments, because the rules to be applied are prescriptive and their terms are general. That does not leave us without resort to reason in the form of human reasonableness, which is enough.

The effort to transcend the limits of human reason in the workings of the law has a benign purpose. It is to ensure that the law's moral authority and power to compel are not

[161]

misused and to achieve justice in the small affairs that constitute most lives even as we try to do in matters of general social concern. Confidence that there is a source of true justice and that it is attainable has often provided a bulwark against human iniquity or weakness and may sustain the effort to achieve the justice that is within our grasp. Transcendental verities have also, however, swept aside doubts that a more cautious and self-consciously human understanding would have respected. Commitment to a just cause ought not require an infallible proof in advance, lest conviction be mistaken for proof and further deliberation be thwarted. The law especially, because it touches all one's life and for most human purposes is final, has need of incertitudes even as it aspires to clarify its vision of the good. Reliance on the human capacity to reflect and deliberate about human ends and how to achieve them does not yield the truths of abstract reason or empirical science. It gives no haven from doubt and requires us continually to evaluate and reconsider our conclusions and to be alert to the possibility of error. For just those reasons, it is our safest, least treacherous path to a just social order.

APPENDIX A

Note on Analogical Reasoning

The process of analogical reasoning depends on the perception of similarities and the ability to sort them according to one's purpose. With that in mind, study in depth of analogical reasoning might begin with some consideration of the group of related ontological, epistemological, and linguistic issues that are commonly grouped together as "the problem of universals," which goes back in the philosophic literature to Plato and Aristotle. Crudely defined, a universal is any *category*: man, woman, or person, as opposed to my friend Jenni; screwdriver or tool, as opposed to the screwdriver that I left on my workbench; race or running, as opposed to the 10K race along Main Street last Saturday morning; anger or emotion, as opposed to Jim's anger when Paul laughed. Framed ontologically, the general issue has to do with the existence of "natural kinds" (called by Plato "Forms" or "Ideas") corresponding to general terms. Even to state the issue that way raises difficulties. One can certainly write an essay about the category of entertainers who are called clowns. But does the *category* of clowns exist in any stronger sense than that, as an actual part of what there is? If so, it assuredly does not exist in just the same way that the particular clowns one sees at the circus exist. Framed epistemologically, the general issue is how we come to know and understand general terms like "clown" in a way that enables us to use them. For we surely do not acquire such knowledge by perceiving categories themselves, as we see and hear a particular clown. Framed linguistically, the general issue is how to give an adequate account of the function and operation of general terms in language. Whether the issue is posed ontologically, epistemologically, or linguistically, the universal that is at stake is, in some sense, the same.

There is a good brief introduction to the problem of universals in W. V. Quine's essay, *Natural Kinds*, in W. V. Quine, *Ontological Relativity and Other Essays* 114 (1969), reprinted in Hilary Kornblith, ed., *Naturalizing Epistemology* 57 (2d ed. 1994). Hilary Staniland, *Universals* (1972) is a short and accessible general survey, which includes material about the ontological formulations of the problem in Plato and Aristotle and the epistemological formulations of the British empiricists (Locke, Berkeley, Hume) as well as more recent work.

Appendix A. Note on Analogical Reasoning

There is also a useful bibliography. Richard I. Aaron, *The Theory of Universals* (2d ed. 1967) is a more elaborate and penetrating study, also with historical material. There are excellent topical essays at a high level and a selective bibliography in Michael J. Loux, ed., *Universals and Particulars: Readings in Ontology* (Notre Dame Press ed. 1976). Recently, the problem of universals has been overtaken, if not taken over, by work on categorization in the field of cognitive psychology, as to which, see below.

Since about 1970, often stimulated by interest in learning and instructional methods or in artificial intelligence and computer science, there has been extensive experimentation and analysis of analogical reasoning in cognitive and developmental psychology. One set of studies has examined the conditions in which an analogy is likely to be a reliable basis for a conclusion – what was discussed generally in the text under the rubric of "relevance" – and another has examined the cognitive conditions for the formation and recognition of an analogy. The studies indicate that similarities between a source and target are more likely to contribute to an analogy that is effective in both respects if they are systematic, that is pervasive and consistent, and not merely discrete "surface" resemblances, like the same color or shape. For a survey of work of this kind, see Deidre Gentner, *The Mechanisms of Analogical Learning*, in Stella Vosniadou & Andrew Ortony, eds., *Similarity and Analogical Reasoning* 199–241 (1989). The results of such studies have been applied extensively in computational models of analogical reasoning used to develop computer programs. They have been applied also in the development of methods of classroom teaching generally.

For a highly accessible general introduction to the subject of analogical reasoning, see Keith J. Holyoak & Paul Thagard, *Mental Leaps: Analogy in Creative Thought* (1995). Informative essays on many topics are collected in David H. Helman, ed., *Analogical Reasoning* (1988) and Vosniadou & Ortony, above. Both collections contain essays describing and evaluating computational models of analogical reasoning.

A good deal of attention has been given to the development of analogical reasoning in children. Experiments are described and the results discussed in Usha Goswami, *Analogical Reasoning in Children* (1992) and in Ann L. Brown, *Analogical Learning and Transfer: What Develops?* in Vosniadou & Ortony, above, at 369–412. Goswami presents persuasive experimental evidence for the theses that the capacity for analogical reasoning is present very early and that its development depends on the acquisition of conceptual and systematic knowledge beyond simple perceptual resemblances.

Analogy and metaphor have much in common. The difference between them might be described (metaphorically) as the distance between the things being compared. Whereas the similarities on which an analogy is based are likely to be evident once they are pointed out and the strength of an analogy depends on the relevance of the similarities to the matter in question, the similarity that supports a metaphor may be elusive; the metaphor's strength may depend on the striking juxtaposition of things that are at first glance unlike one another. Many of the issues about analogy and metaphor that are studied in epistemology, linguistics, and cognitive psychology overlap. A useful collection of essays about metaphor, which brings together work from the different fields and contains a lengthy bibliography, is Andrew Ortony, ed., *Metaphor and Thought* (2d ed. 1993).

Another kind of study in cognitive psychology has explored the pervasive presence of analogy and metaphor in thought and language, not as a deliberate step in reasoning and communication but as deeply embedded in the categories by which we understand and describe our experience. "[A]nalogical and metaphorical projection is pervasive in human understanding at a level of meaning and reasoning below that of propositional relations." Mark Johnson, *Some Constraints on Embodied Analogical Understanding*, in Helman, above, at 1, 26 (1988). "Our explicit reflective analogizing typically rests upon a massive interconnected web of experientially embodied analogical connections and processes of which we are seldom aware." Id. at 39. Such studies provide persuasive evidence that general terms are not more or less accurate (objective) abstract representations of what they describe, independent of the circumstances of their user and use; rather, they comprise a richly embodied conceptual system that depends heavily not only on our physical selves but on every aspect – psychological, social, historical, linguistic – of our humanness. So, it is argued, general terms are not susceptible to logical transformations in the manner of deduction but have to be analyzed contextually. And, it follows, the goal cannot be certain truth, any departure from which is unacceptable, but must be a more limited, situational kind of reasonableness that reflects this embedded humanness. The leading work in this area has been done by George Lakoff and Mark Johnson. See George Lakoff, *Women, Fire, and Dangerous Things* (1987); George Lakoff & Mark Johnson, *Metaphors We Live By* (1980); Mark Johnson, *The Body in the Mind* (1987). Mark Johnson, *Moral Imagination* (1993) is a powerful study of the implications of this work for moral philosophy and ethics. Steven L. Winter, *A Clearing in the Forest* (2001) applies this work in the field of law with striking results.

Biographical Notes

Lawrence A. Alexander, Professor, University of San Diego School of Law. Writes extensively on jurisprudence and constitutional law.

Scott Brewer, Professor, Harvard Law School. Writes on jurisprudence and evidence.

Ronald Dworkin, Professor of Jurisprudence, University of Oxford, and Professor, New York University School of Law. Writes extensively on jurisprudence. Works include *Taking Rights Seriously* (1977), *A Matter of Principle* (1984), and *Law's Empire* (1986).

Melvin A. Eisenberg, Professor, University of California, Berkeley, School of Law. Writes on contracts, corporations, and legal process. Works include *The Nature of the Common Law* (1988).

Legal Reason

Lon L. Fuller (1902–1978), Professor, Harvard Law School. Wrote extensively on jurisprudence, legal theory, and contracts. Principal jurisprudential works include *The Law in Quest of Itself* (1940), *The Morality of Law* (rev'd ed. 1977), and *Positivism and Fidelity to Law – A Reply to Professor Hart*, 71 Harv. L. Rev. 630 (1958).

R. Kent Greenawalt, Professor, Columbia Law School. Writes extensively on jurisprudence, constitutional law, and the First Amendment. Works include *Conflicts of Law and Morality* (1987), *Law and Objectivity* (1992), and *Private Consciences and Public Reasons* (1995).

H(erbert) L(ionel) A(dolphus) Hart (1907–1993), Professor of Jurisprudence, Oxford University. Wrote extensively on jurisprudence. Works include *The Concept of Law* (2d ed. 1994); *Law, Liberty and Morality* (1963), *Punishment and Responsibility* (1968), and *Positivism and the Separation of Law and Morals*, 71 Harv. L. Rev. 593 (1958).

Oliver Wendell Holmes, Jr. (1841–1935), Professor of Law, Harvard Law School; Chief Justice, Supreme Judicial Court of Massachusetts; Justice of the Supreme Court of the United States (1902–1932). Wrote extensively on many legal subjects, including jurisprudence and legal theory. Works include *The Common Law* (1881) and *The Path of the Law*, 10 Harv. L. Rev. 457 (1897).

Edward Hirsch Levi (1911–2000), Professor of Law and Dean, The University of Chicago Law School; President, The University of Chicago; Attorney General of the United States under Presidents Ford and Carter, 1975–77. Principal jurisprudential work is *An Introduction to Legal Reasoning* (1949).

Neil MacCormick, Regius Professor of Public Law, Edinburgh University; Member for Scotland, European Parliament. Writes principally on jurisprudence, legal theory, and constitutional law. Works include *Legal Reasoning and Legal Theory* (1978).

Charles Peirce (1839–1914), American philosopher and logician, founder of the philosophical school of pragmatism. Wrote principally on logic but extensively also on many other subjects. Writings are collected in *The Collected Papers of Charles Sanders Peirce*, vols. 1–6 (C. Hartshorne & P. Weiss, eds., 1931–35), vols. 7–8 (A. Burks, ed., 1958).

Richard A. Posner, Judge of the United States Court of Appeals for the Seventh Circuit; Lecturer at The University of Chicago Law School. Writes extensively on many legal subjects, notably in the field of law and economics (*Economic Analysis of Law* [6th ed. 2003]). Jurisprudential works include *The Problems of Jurisprudence* (1990), *Overcoming Law* (1995), and *Law, Pragmatism, and Democracy* (2003).

Willard Van Orman Quine, Professor of Philosophy (retired), Harvard University. Writes extensively on philosophy, logic, and language. Works include *From a Logical Point of View* (2d ed. 1961), *Word and Object* (1960), and *Ontological Relativity and*

Other Essays (1969). Selections from his writings are collected in *Quintessence* (R.F. Gibson, ed., 2004).

Cass R. Sunstein, Professor of Law, The University of Chicago Law School. Writes extensively on jurisprudence, constitutional law, and administrative law. Principal jurisprudential work is *Legal Reasoning and Political Conflict* (1996).

Peter Westen, Professor, University of Michigan Law School. Writes extensively on jurisprudence and criminal law and procedure.

Notes

Introduction

1. See, in addition to books cited elsewhere, Ruggero J. Aldisert, *Logic for Lawyers* (3d ed. 1997); Robert Alexy, *A Theory of Legal Argumentation* (R. Adler & N. MacCormick, trans.) (1989); Fernando Atria, *On Law and Legal Reasoning* (2001); Steven J. Burton, *An Introduction to Law and Legal Reasoning* (2d ed. 1995); Martin P. Golding, *Legal Reasoning* (1984); Peter Goodrich, *Legal Discourse* (1987); William Read, *Legal Thinking* (1986); Elias E. Savellos, *Reasoning and the Law* (2001); Clarence Morris, *How Lawyers Think* (1994); Kenneth J. Vandevelde, *Thinking Like a Lawyer: An Introduction to Legal Reasoning* (1996). For a strong statement that "thinking like a lawyer is just ordinary forms of thinking clearly and well," see Larry Alexander, *The Banality of Legal Reasoning*, 73 Notre Dame L. Rev. 517, 517 (1998).
2. The strongest recent claim that there is a "right answer" has been made by Ronald Dworkin. See Ronald Dworkin, *Hard Cases*, 88 Harv. L. Rev. 1057 (1975), reprinted in Ronald Dworkin, *Taking Rights Seriously* 81–130 (1977); Ronald Dworkin, *No Right Answer?*, 53 N.Y.U. L. Rev. 1 (1978), reprinted in Ronald Dworkin, *A Matter of Principle*, 119–145 (1985).
3. Dworkin, *Taking Rights Seriously*, note 2, at 87, 88.
4. Id. at 117.

5. Ronald Dworkin, *In Praise of Theory*, 29 Ariz. St. L. J. 353, 357 (1997).
6. Dworkin, *Taking Rights Seriously*, note 2, at 105.
7. Edward H. Levi, *An Introduction to Legal Reasoning* 1 (1949).
8. Richard Posner, *Overcoming Law* 177, 519–520 (1995).
9. See, e.g., H.L.A. Hart, *Positivism and the Separation of Law and Morals*, 71 Harv. L. Rev. 593, 613 (1958); Lon L. Fuller, *Positivism and Fidelity to Law – A Reply to Professor Hart*, 71 Harv. L. Rev. 630, 659–660 (1958).
10. For a good introduction to the debate, see Antonin Scalia, *A Matter of Interpretation* (1997), which contains an essay by the Justice, a leading exponent of "originalism," as to which see pp. 156–157, and five commentaries. Ronald Dworkin's much-discussed interpretive theory is set forth in Dworkin, *A Matter of Principle*, note 2, at 119–177, and Ronald Dworkin, *Law's Empire* 45–86 (1986). William N. Eskridge, Jr., *Dynamic Statutory Interpretation* (1994), provides a thorough discussion of legal interpretation, with many references.
11. Cass Sunstein, *Legal Reasoning and Political Conflict* 75 (1996).
12. See Scott Brewer, *Exemplary Reasoning: Semantics, Pragmatics, and the Rational Force of Legal Argument by Analogy*, 109 Harv. L. Rev. 923 (1996).
13. 151 N.Y. 163 (1896).
14. *Adams* is discussed in connection with analogical legal argument in Brewer, note 12, at 1003–1006, 1013–1016, and in Golding, note 1, at 46–48, 102–110.
15. *Buck v. Jewell-LaSalle Realty Co.*, 283 U.S. 191 (1931); *Fortnightly Corp. v. United Artists Television, Inc.*, 392 U.S. 390 (1968); *Teleprompter Corp. v. Columbia Broadcasting System, Inc.*, 415 U.S. 394 (1974); *Twentieth Century Music Corp. v. Aiken*, 422 U.S. 151 (1975).
16. 277 U.S. 438 (1928).
17. 389 U.S. 347 (1967).

Chapter One. Analogy and Inductive and Deductive Reasoning

1. Scott Brewer, *Exemplary Reasoning: Semantics, Pragmatics, and the Rational Force of Legal Argument by Analogy*, 109 Harv. L. Rev. 923, 934 (1996).
2. Id. at 928.
3. Id. at 962.
4. See *United States v. Chadwick*, 433 U.S. 1 (1977).
5. See Brewer, note 1, at 945–949. There are references to abduction throughout Peirce's writings. For extended discussions, see 5–6 *The*

Collected Papers of Charles Sanders Peirce 5.180–212, 5.272–82, 5.590–604, 6.526–36 (C. Hartshorne & P. Weiss, eds., 1931–35); 7 *The Collected Papers of Charles Sanders Peirce* 7.218–22 (A. Burks, ed., 1958) (numbers refer to paragraphs). For a general account of Peirce's theory of abduction, which developed over time, see K. T. Fann, *Peirce's Theory of Abduction* (1970).

6. See Fann, note 5, at 1–5.
7. Brewer, note 1, at 962.
8. Id.
9. Id.
10. Id. at 963.
11. Id.
12. Id. at 949.
13. Id. at 967.
14. Id. at 933, 953–954.
15. Id. at 933, 952–953.
16. Id. at 952.
17. Cass Sunstein, *Legal Reasoning and Political Conflict* 69 (1996).
18. Id. at 68.
19. Id. at 35.
20. Edward H. Levi, *An Introduction to Legal Reasoning* 5 (1949).
21. Sunstein, note 17, at 75.
22. Brewer, note 1, at 933.
23. Sunstein, note 17, at 65.
24. Id.
25. Brewer, note 1, at 933, 952–953.
26. Brewer, note 1, at 954, 964.
27. Id. at 933.
28. Id.
29. Id. at 1027.
30. See id. at 991–94, 1003–1006.
31. Id. at 965.

Chapter Two. Steamboats, Broadcast Transmissions, and Electronic Eavesdropping

1. *Adams v. New Jersey Steamboat Co.*, 151 N.Y. 163 (1896).
2. Id. at 166.
3. Id. at 167.

4. Id.
5. Id.
6. Id. at 168–170.
7. Id. at 170.
8. Id.
9. Id. at 168–169.
10. Id. at 169.
11. Scott Brewer, *Exemplary Reasoning: Semantics, Pragmatics, and the Rational Force of Reasoning by Analogy*, 109 Harv. L. Rev. 923, 1003–1006, 1013–1016 (1996).
12. See id. at 1006–1016.
13. Act of March 4, 1909, Ch. 320, §1(e), 35 Stat. 1075.
14. 283 U.S. 191 (1931).
15. Id. at 199 (footnote omitted).
16. Id. at 199 n.7.
17. Id. at 201 (footnote omitted).
18. Id. at 199.
19. Id. at 201 n.10.
20. 392 U.S. 390 (1968).
21. Id. at 395–396.
22. Id. at 399.
23. Id. (footnote omitted).
24. Id. at 400.
25. Id. at 401.
26. Id. at 397 n.18.
27. 415 U.S. 394 (1974).
28. Id. at 403–404.
29. Id. at 407–411.
30. Id. at 403 (quoting *Fortnightly*, 392 U.S. at 398).
31. Id. at 408.
32. Id. at 414 n.15.
33. Id. at 414 (footnote omitted).
34. Id. at 415 (Blackmun, J., dissenting).
35. Id. at 417.
36. Id. at 422.
37. 422 U.S. 151 (1975).
38. Id. at 159.
39. *Fortnightly*, 392 U.S. at 395.
40. *Olmstead v. United States*, 277 U.S. 438 (1928).
41. Id. at 464.

42. Id.
43. Id. at 464–465.
44. Id. at 466.
45. Id. at 465–466.
46. Id. at 478 (Brandeis, J., dissenting).
47. Id. at 487 (Butler, J., dissenting).
48. 389 U.S. 347 (1967).
49. *Silverman v. United States*, 365 U.S. 505 (1961).
50. *Katz*, 389 U.S. at 353.
51. Id. at 365 (Black, J., dissenting).
52. Id. at 366.
53. Id. at 373.
54. Id. at 352 (footnotes omitted).
55. Id. at 359 (Douglas, J., concurring), 362 (White, J., concurring).
56. Id. at 353.
57. Id. at 350–351 (footnotes omitted).
58. *Olmstead*, 277 U.S. at 464 (emphasis supplied).
59. *Katz*, 389 U.S. at 351–352 (emphasis supplied).
60. Id. at 352.

Chapter Three. Analogical Legal Reasoning

1. *Adams v. New Jersey Steamboat Co.*, 151 N.Y. 163, 167, 170 (1896).
2. Id. at 167.
3. *Silverman v. United States*, 365 U.S. 505 (1961).
4. *Goldman v. United States*, 316 U.S. 129 (1942).
5. *Silverman*, 365 U.S. at 509, 511.
6. Id. at 513.
7. *Katz v. United States*, 389 U.S. 347, 348, 352 (1967).
8. Id. at 352–353.
9. See, e.g., *Rakas v. Illinois*, 439 U.S. 128, 144 n.12 (1978); *Minnesota v. Carter*, 525 U.S. 83, 88–91 (1998).
10. Morton J. Horwitz, *The Transformation of American Law 1870–1960*, 203 (1992) (footnote omitted).
11. See W. V. Quine, *Natural Kinds*, in W. V. Quine, *Ontological Relativity and Other Essays* 114, 135–138 (1969), reprinted in Hilary Kornblith, ed., *Naturalizing Epistemology* 57, 72–74 (2d ed. 1994).
12. Peter Westen, *On "Confusing Ideas": Reply*, 91 Yale L.J. 1153, 1163 (1982) (footnote omitted).

13. See *Rakas v. Illinois*, 439 U.S. 128 (1978) (automobile); *Minnesota v. Carter*, 525 U.S. 83 (1998) (apartment); *California v. Ciraolo*, 476 U.S. 207 (1986) (yard); *California v. Greenwood*, 486 U.S. 35 (1988) (trash).
14. Richard A. Posner, *Law, Pragmatism, and Democracy* 49, 53, 52 (2003).
15. See generally id. at 57–96.
16. Id. at 61.
17. Id. at 13, 64.
18. See, e.g., Richard A Posner, *The Problematics of Moral and Legal Theory*, 111 Harv. L. Rev. 1638 (1998).
19. Posner, note 14, at 82.
20. See id. at 158–212.

Chapter Four. Analogical Reasoning, Legal Education, and the Law

1. Usha Goswami, *Analogical Reasoning in Children* 13, 99–115 (1992); Keith J. Holyoak & Paul Thagard, *Mental Leaps* 75–100 (1995). On animals, see Holyoak & Thagard, at 39–73.
2. Goswami, note 1, at 35. See generally id. at 35–40.
3. Goswami, note 1, at 3–4, 17–19.
4. Id. at 6–9.
5. Id. at 19.
6. See id. at 35–98.
7. Goswami, note 1, at 14. See id. at 93–97.
8. See Margaret Goldsmith, *The Road to Penicillin* 150–156 (1946).
9. The class is described in some detail in Samuel F. Batchelder, *Christopher C. Langdell*, 18 Green Bag 437 (1906), which also gives information about Langdell's youth, education, and professional life before he joined the faculty.
10. For an insightful study of Langdell's jurisprudence, see Thomas C. Grey, *Langdell's Orthodoxy*, 45 U. Pitt. L. Rev. 1 (1983).
11. See, e.g., Jerome Frank, *Law and the Modern Mind* 127–158 (1970); Roscoe Pound, *Mechanical Jurisprudence*, 8 Colum. L. Rev. 605 (1908).
12. Robert Stevens, *Two Cheers for 1870: The American Law School*, in Donald Fleming and Bernard Bailyn, eds., *Law in American History* (5 Perspectives in American History) 403, 426–427 (1971).
13. William P. LaPiana, *Logic and Experience* 55–70 (1994). Langdell's methodology, especially its assumption that legal science is a deductive system akin to mathematics, is traced back to the past in M. H. Hoeflich,

Law & Geometry: Legal Science from Leibniz to Langdell, 30 Am. J. Legal Hist. 95 (1986).

14. See Grey, note 8, at 20–27.

15. See, e.g., Karl Llewellyn's famous juxtaposition of opposed canons of statutory construction in Karl N. Llewellyn, *Remarks on the Theory of Appellate Decision and the Rules or Canons About How Statutes Are To Be Construed*, 3 Vand. L. Rev. 395 (1950). Llewellyn's more complete (and not unfavorable) view of appellate decision making is set forth in Karl N. Llewellyn, *The Common Law Tradition* (1960). See also Clare Dalton, *An Essay in the Deconstruction of Contract Doctrine*, 94 Yale L.J. 997 (1985). For the history of Legal Realism in the United States, see Morton J. Horwitz, *The Transformation of American Law 1870–1960*, 169–246 (1992). There is an insightful description of the legal realist movement in Lon L. Fuller, *American Legal Realism*, 82 U. Pa. L. Rev. 429 (1934). Selections of the writings of the Legal Realists are found in William W. Fisher III, Morton J. Horwitz, & Thomas A. Reed, eds., *American Legal Realism* (1993). On Critical Legal Studies, see Roberto Mangabeira Unger, *The Critical Legal Studies Movement* (1986). For a bibliography, see Duncan Kennedy & Karl E. Klare, *A Bibliography of Critical Legal Studies*, 94 Yale L. J. 461 (1984).

16. Batchelder, note 9, at 440.

17. Joseph Raz, *The Authority of Law* 210–229 (1979) provides a good general overview. For a careful exposition of the various meanings of the rule of law in jurisprudential and especially constitutional debate, see Richard H. Fallon, Jr., *"The Rule of Law" as a Concept in Constitutional Discourse*, 97 Colum. L. Rev. 1 (1997).

18. See Lon L. Fuller, *The Morality of Law* (rev. ed. 1977). Fuller's extended discussion of "the morality that makes law possible," id. at 33, may itself be regarded as a statement of what the rule of law requires. See id. at 33–94.

19. Scott Brewer, *Exemplary Reasoning: Semantics, Pragmatics, and the Rational Force of Legal Argument by Analogy*, 109 Harv. L. Rev. 923, 934 (1996).

20. Richard A. Posner, *Legal Scholarship Today*, 45 Stan. L. Rev. 1647, 1654 (1993).

21. *Brown v. Allen*, 344 U.S. 443, 540 (1953) (concurring opinion.)

22. See Lloyd L. Weinreb, *Natural Law and Justice* 15–66, 224–65 (1987).

23. See, e.g., John Finnis, *Natural Law and Natural Rights* (1980). See generally Weinreb, note 22, at 101–126.

24. On the debate between natural law and legal positivism, see Weinreb, note 22 above, at 97–101, 259–265.
25. *Adamson v. California*, 332 U.S. 46, 68 (1947) (dissenting opinion).
26. Id. at 66 (concurring opinion).
27. See id. at 66–68.
28. Justice Black's historical argument is contained in an appendix to his opinion in *Adamson*, note 25, at 92. For Justice Frankfurter's view, see id. at 62–67. For a thorough response to Justice Black's historical argument, see Charles Fairman, *Does the Fourteenth Amendment Incorporate the Bill of Rights?*, 2 Stan. L. Rev. 5 (1949), which rejects Black's conclusion.
29. See, in addition to *Adamson*, note 25, at 69, 90, *Rochin v. California*, 342 U.S. 165, 174–177 (1952) (Black, J., concurring). For a later tirade by Black against the "natural law" approach, see *Griswold v. Connecticut*, 381 U.S. 479, 511–513, 522–524 (1965) (Black, J., dissenting). Justice Souter uses the label of "natural law" pejoratively, on an entirely different subject, in *Alden v. Maine*, 527 U.S. 706, 763 (1999) (dissenting opinion). See id. at 763–798. The majority rejected Justice Souter's characterization. See id. at 758–789.
30. *Adamson*, note 25, at 65, 67–68 (Frankfurter, J., concurring); *Rochin*, note 29, at 169–172.

Index

Index

Index

legal formalism, 37, 116. *See also*
"mechanical jurisprudence"
"legal science" 140–142, 149
legal positivism, 14, 81n., 155,
157–158
convention (*nomos*), 153
Protagoras, 153n.
Sophists, 153
Legal Realism, 8n., 14, 81n., 139, 142
legal reasoning, 1–5, 12–15, 38, 66,
77–103, 107, 123–124. *See also*
adjudication, analogical
reasoning, law
practical reasoning compared,
74–77
pyramidal structure, 5–6, 7, 134
search for certainty, 13–14, 17, 162
use of analogy, 4–5, 39, 123–124
"legal science," 140–142, 149
legislation, 1, 36, 77, 118, 120
Levi, Edward, 9, 14, 30–31, 67, 107n.,
170
liability for loss
innkeeper, 42–45, 61, 83–84, 93–94,
133, 134, 137
railroad sleeping car operator,
42–43, 133
steamboat operator, 42–45, 61,
83–84, 133, 137

MacCormick, Neil, 11, 171
MacPherson v. Buick Motor Co., 100n.
Marbury v. Madison, 147n.
Marshall, John, 147
"mechanical jurisprudence" 104–105,
139. *See also* legal formalism, legal
reasoning
metaphor, 109n., 111–112, 166–167
Miranda v. Arizona, 78n., 88n., 94n.

natural law, 14, 38, 81n., 152n., 153,
154. *See also* constitutional
interpretation
normative natural order, 153

Nazism, 14, 155–156
normative natural order, 153. *See also*
natural law
Plato, 153
Providence, 154

Olmstead v. United States, 15, 54–57,
60, 62, 84–85, 86, 99, 100, 134,
135
originalism, 156–157

Parker v. State, 89n.
Peirce, Charles, 22–23, 171. *See also*
abduction
Plato, 153
Posner, Richard, 9–10, 11, 67, 108n.,
117–121, 150, 171
"everyday pragmatism,"
118–119
law and economics, 118n.
rule of law, 119
theory of adjudication, 5,
118–121
Protagoras, 153n.

Quine, Willard Van Orman, 171

Rakas v. Illinois, 101n.
restatements, 75
rules. *See also* legal reasoning
and principles, 5n., 106–107
and standards, 6n.
rule of law, 13, 17, 34–37, 118, 135,
146–152. *See also* Posner,
Richard
rule of recognition, 39n.

Sherlock Holmes, 22n.
similarity, 123–128, 130. *See also*,
analogy, universals
causal relations, 128–130
normative relations, 131–132
Sophists, 153
Stone, Harlan Fiske, 56

Index